A Powys Anthology

Dewi Roberts

ISBN: 0-86381-840-4

First published in June 2003 by
Gwasg Carreg Gwalch, 12 Iard yr Orsaf, Llanrwst, Wales LL26 0EH
☎ 01492 642031   📠 01492 641502
📧 books@carreg-gwalch.co.uk   website: www.carreg-gwalch.co.uk

A POWYS ANTHOLOGY

A Powys Anthology

Introduction 10
Acknowledgements 13

Topography

Peter Porter: Magica Sympathia 16
J.E. Lloyd: The Eden of Wales from 'A History of Wales' 17
W.H. Potts: From Llangurig to Rhayader from 'Roaming Down the
    Wye' 18
Pauline Phillips: Powys Paradwys Cymru from 'A View of Old
    Montgomeryshire' 18
Philip Carr: Hirnant, Powys 19
Rayner Heppenstall: Climbing Towards Machynlleth from
    'The Woodshed' 20
Iorwerth Peate: Meallow Beauty from the Journal of the
    Anthropological Society 21
Roland Mathias: A Stare from the Mountain 22
George Lyttleton: An Account of a Journey into Wales 23
Daniel Defoe: 'A Good Fashionable Place' from 'A Tour Through
    the Whole Island of Great Britain' 24
George Borrow: 'The Grand Cataract' from 'Wild Wales' 25
Robert Roberts: 'Debatable Land' from 'The Life and Opinions of
    a Wandering Scholar' 25
Alwyn D. Rees: A Pioneering Study from 'Life in a Welsh Countryside' ... 26
Huw Jones: The Gateway to Wales from an article which appeared
    in 'Poetry Wales' 27
R.S. Thomas: Manafon from 'Selected Prose', edited by Sandra Anstey ... 28
Alun Llewelyn-Williams: 'Damn English!' from 'The Light in the
    Gloom', translated by Joseph P. Clancy 29
Richard Hall: Crickhowel 30
Walter Savage Landor: Llanthony 30
Robert Gibbings: Pumlumon from 'Coming Down the Wye' 31
Graham Thomas: At Llyn Clywedog 32
Francis Brett Young: Forest Fawr from 'The House Under the Water' ... 33
Phil Carradice: In the Garden at Bronllys 35
Huw Jones: Llandrindod Wells, November 36
Christopher Meredith: On Hay Bridge 37

Julie Rainsbury: Powis Castle 38
John Moore: The Road to Montgomery from 'The Welsh Marches' 39
Norman Schwenk: Gregynog Hall 39
T. Harri Jones: Llanafan Unrevisitied 40
Eiluned Lewis: The River 41
Francis Brett Young: The Teme from 'The Island' 42
Ruth Bidgood: Little of Distinction 43
Gloria Evans Davies: Sheep on the Brecon Hills 44
Joyce Herbert: Usk 45
Christopher Meredith: By Bronllys Castle 46
Bryan Martin Davies: Night on the Dyke, translated by Grahame
    Davies 47
Ruth Bidgood: Llanfihangel 48
Douglas A. Bassett: The Llanbryn-mair Tradition from the text of
    a lecture delivered to the Honourable Society of Cymmrodorion 49
Anthony Bailey: On Pen-y-Fan from 'A Walk Through Wales' 50

People

John Cowper Powys: 'Y Crach' from 'Owen Glendower' 51
Gwerful Mechain: Asking for a Harp 52
Richard Williams: 'The Bountiful' from 'Montgomeryshire Worthies' 54
John Donne: The Primrose 55
Philip Yorke: Portrait of a Country Gentleman from 'Royal Tribes' 56
David Bell: Shrouded in Mystery from 'The Artist in Wales' 58
Jospeh Hucks: 'Contemptible and Insignificant' from 'A Pedestrian Tour
    Through North Wales', edited by Alun Jones and William Tydeman 59
Walter Davies: The Permanency of the Language from 'The
    English Works of Rev. Walter Davies', edited by Silvan Evans 60
Iorwerth Peate: The Genius of the Mountains from 'Sylfeini' 61
Iorwerth Peate: Nant yr Eira, translated by Joseph P. Clancy 62
D.J. Williams: Catherine Lloyd, translated by R. Gerallt Jones
    and included in 'The Penguin Book of Welsh Short Stories',
    edited by Alun Richards 63
Margiad Evans: A Love Story from 'Country Dance' 64
Eiluned Lewis: In the Hayfield from 'Dew in the Grass' 66
James Hanley: My Village from an essay in the journal 'Wales' 67
Islwyn Ffowc Elis: Cysgod y Cryman (Shadow of the Sickle),
    translated by Meic Stephens 68

R.S. Thomas: An Unanswered Question from 'Selected Prose', edited by Sandra Anstey 69

Harri Webb: The Next Village to Manafon 70

Raymond Garlick: Saunders Lewis at Newtown 71

Nigel Jenkins: On the Border, Llanymynech 72

Ruth Bidgood: Emu's Egg 74

Robert Roberts: 'A Malignant Power' from 'The Life and Opinions of a Wandering Scholar' 75

Tobias Smollet: Brambleton Hall from 'The Expedition of Humphrey Clinker' 76

P.B. Shelley: Shelley at Cwm Elan from 'The Letters of Percy Bysshe Shelley', edited by F.L. Jones 77

Hilda Vaughan: Parted from 'A Thing of Nought' 78

Thoresby Jones: An Extraordinary Vicar from 'Welsh Border Country' ... 80

Francis Kilvert: Kilvert Visits the Solitary from the Diary 80

Caroline Price: The Radnor Hermit 82

A. Scriven: 'The Dartmoor Shepherd' from 'The Dartmoor Shepherd: Fifty Years in Prison' 84

David Constantine: The Pathos In It from 'Davies' 85

Iorwerth Peate: The Lost Kingdom 86

Geraint Goodwin: Churning from 'The Heyday of the Blood' 87

Alwyn D. Rees: The Social Mix of Llanfihangel from 'Life in a Welsh Countryside' 88

Andrew Morrison: Border Lambing 89

John Idris Jones: The Magic of Mr Smith from 'Berwyn Christmas' included in 'Christmas in Wales' edited by Dewi Roberts 92

John Hillaby: A Nobody-About Place from 'Journey Through Britain' .. 93

Bruce Chatwin: A Radnorshire Family from 'On the Black Hill' 94

W.G. Sebald: Llanwddyn Submerged from 'Austerlitz' 95

Christopher Meredith: My son on Castell Dinas 97

Siân James: Glyn from 'And Perhaps More' included in 'Outside Paradise' 98

Alice Thomas Ellis: A Lousy Day from 'Unexplained Laughter' 99

Leslie Norris: A small war 100

John Davies: Border incident 101

History

The Mabinogion: The Dream of Rhonabwy, translated by Charlotte Guest 103

Tacitus: The Last Stand of Caractacus from 'The Annals of Ancient Rome', translated by Michael Grant 105

Brian Morris: Beacons 107

Helen Cresswell: Haunted Country from 'Stonestruck' 108

Grahame Davies: Guilty, translated by the poet 109

Merryn Williams: Tretower Court 109

Pauline Phillips: Continuity and Persistence from 'A View of Montgomeryshire' 110

Walter Davies: Llywarch Hen from 'The English Works of Walter Davies', edited by Silvan Evans 110

Anon: Cynddylan's Hall, translated by Tony Conran 111

Richard Williams: 'The Only Hope' from 'Montgomeryshire Worthies' ... 112

S. Barring Gould: 'The Siege of Pains Castle' from 'A Book of South Wales' 115

Walter Scott: Born Invulnerable from 'The Betrothed' 116

Jan Morris and Twm Morys: A Machynlleth Triad 119

George Borrow: A Thoroughly Welsh Town from 'Wild Wales' 120

Iolo Goch: Owain Glyndŵr's Court, translated by Dafydd Johnson ... 120

George Borrow: Sycharth from 'Wild Wales' 122

David Rees: A meeting on Long Mountain from 'The Son of Prophecy' ... 124

Lord Edward Herbert: A Just Man from 'Autobiography' 124

S. Baring Gould: An Abortive Plot from 'A Book of South Wales' 125

S. Baring Gould: A Devilish Woman from 'A Book of South Wales' ... 126

Churchyard inscription: King of Powys 127

Melvin Humphreys: The Crises of Community; Montgomeryshire 127

Brian Waters: Sir John Pryce from 'Severn Stream' 128

W.J. Lewis: Mining from 'Lead Mining in Wales' 129

Robert Parry: An address to Newtown 129

J. Geraint Jenkins: Wool from 'The Welsh Woollen Industry' 130

Samuel Roberts: Samuel Roberts and the Baron from 'Gweithiau Samuel Roberts', translated by Grahame Davies 130

Edward Hamer: Rebellion at Llanidloes from 'A Brief Account of the Chartist Outbreak in Llanidloes in the year 1839' 132

G.D.H. Cole: Robert Owen from 'Robert Owen' 134

Robert Owen: Character Forming from 'The Life of Robert Owen' 135

Herbert Williams: Davies the Ocean from 'Davies the Ocean' 136

Eirene White: A Lasting Memorial from 'The Ladies of Gregynog' 137

Alun D.W. Owen: Without Fears or Tears from 'A Montgomeryshire Youth' 138

Michael Martholomew-Biggs: Crash at Pennant Melangell, 1943 138

Cledwyn Hughes: The Mowing Machine from 'The House in the
Cornfield' 139
Ralph Cartright and R.T. Russell: The Welshpool and Llanfair
Railway from 'The Welshpool and Llanfair Light Railway' 140
Stewart Brown: With all my griefs in my arms 141
Alun D.W. Owen: Reflections from 'A Montgomeryshire Youth' 142

Religion

Graham Hartill: Cennau's Bell 144
Sabine Baring-Gould: The Patroness of Hares from 'The Book of
North Wales' 148
Glenda Beagan: Melangell 149
S. Baring Gould and John Fisher: Beuno from 'The Lives of the
British Saints' 151
Huw Jones: Long Mountain 153
Giraldus Cambrensis: Eluned's Feast Day from 'The Journey
Through Wales' 154
Jan Morris: The Silurian from 'Wales: Epic Views of a Small Country' ... 155
Henry Vaughan: The Retreate 156
Siegfried Sassoon: At the Grave of Henry Vaughan 157
Joseph P. Clancy: At the Grave of Henry Vaughan 157
George Herbert: Love 158
O.M. Edwards: William Morgan from 'Wales' 159
R.S. Thomas: Llanrhaeadr-ym-Mochnant 159
Thomas Pennant: The Power of the Cock from 'Tours in Wales' 160
Brian Shuel: The Plygain from 'Guide to Traditional Customs of
Britain' 161
Huw Jones: For the Quakers of Montgomeryshire 162
H.D. Phillips: Persecution from 'The Early Quakers in Wales' 164
Richard Williams: Falsehoods from Montgomeryshire Worthies 165
Jan Morris: Anne Griffiths from 'Wales; Epic Views of a Small
Country' 166
Ann Griffiths: 'Lo, Between the Myrtles' 167
Eric Gill: The Monastery from 'Autobiography' 168
Islwyn Ffowc Elis: Old Tynoro from Cysgod y Cryman (Shadow of
the Sickle) 169

Introduction

The people of the borderlands have lived through bitter periods of conflict with both the Romans and the Saxons. The legacy of existing under the shadow of invasion has resulted, understandably, in a sense of vulnerability on the part of the Welsh of the ancient county of Powys and this has manifested itself in what has been written about the region. In these pages the reader will discover examples from many genres of literature; historical accounts, poetry, fiction, autobiography and other forms of writing.

John Fisher and Sabine Baring Gould write of Beuno's flight westward from Berriew when he heard a Saxon calling his hunting dog on the other side of the Severn. This incident is also the subject of a poem by Huw Jones, the closing lines of which encapsulate something of the essence of border consciousness.

> We migrate with ease across
> borders, carry our culture
> in a suitcase, fear pressing
> like an ingrowing toenail.

Gwallter Mechain writing in the early nineteenth century reflects on the survival of the Welsh language close to Offa's Dyke despite bastard anglicization.

In her novel *Country Dance* Margiad Evans illuminates a world of torn racial allegiances in the nineteenth century. In the novel Sian's father is furious when he learns of his daughter's intention to marry a shopkeeper from Shropshire.

We find an entirely different take on this racial dilemma in W.G. Sebald's haunting novel *Austerlitz*, in which he describes the visit of a Jewish child, who is exiled in Wales, to the Vyrnwy Reservoir. Here he is told of those who have lost their community because of the need for water by the powers-that-be on the other side of the border.

But by no means all the items included are by any means concerned with hostility and estrangement. In four thematic sections the reader will discover a wide range of material from various genres on the history, religion and social life of the former counties of Montgomery, Brecon and Radnor. The authors represented are wide ranging. They include Tacitus, Henry Vaughan, George Herbert, John Donne, Walter Scott, Francis Kilvert and, more recently, R.S. Thomas, Islwyn Ffowc Elis, John Cowper

Powys, Bruce Chatwin and Alice Thomas Ellis.

This anthology really evolved from both my immense interest in the literature of Wales and the fact that, although not born there, my ancestral roots lie firmly in the former county of Montgomery.

Dewi Roberts

Editorial Note

A problem which can face the editor of a Welsh anthology concerns the use of place names.

I have therefore included a selective glossary which includes not only the familiar anglicized names but also the original Welsh ones.

In the case of certain English writers from the past, such as Defoe, and I felt it was appropriate to retain original spellings in order to retain the essential spirit of the pieces.

Glossary of selected place-names in Powys

Brecon (Aberhonddu)
Crickhowell (Crucywel)
Newtown (Y Drenewydd)
Welshpool (Y Trallwng)
Builth Wells (Llanfair-ym-Muallt)
Rhayader (Rhaeadr Gwy)
Montgomery (Trefaldwyn)
Knighton (Trefyclo)
Plynlimon (Pumlumon)
Powis Castle (Castell Coch)
Presteigne (Llanandras)
Llanthony (Llanddewi Nant Hodni)
Kerry (Ceri)
Berriw (Aberriw)
Abermule (Aber-miwl)
Brecon Beacons (Bannau Brycheiniog)
Offa's Dyke (Clawdd Offa)
Lake Vyrnwy (Llyn Fyrnwy)
Radnor (Maesyfed)

Acknowledgements

We wish to thank the following authors, publishers, literary agents and executors for kindly allowing us to reprint items in this anthology. Every effort has been made to contact the owners of copyright but in cases where this has not proved possible we convey our apologies to those concerned.

We are indebted to Seren for permission to reproduce the following poems from titles which have appeared under their imprint – Ruth Bidgood: 'Little of Distinction', 'Llanfihangel' and 'Emu's Egg' from *Selected Poems* (1992); Christopher Meredith: 'On Hay Bridge' and 'My son on Castell Dinas' from *Snaring Heaven* (1990); John Davies: 'Border Incident' from *The Visitor's Book* (1985)

Gwasg Gomer for the following – Huw Jones: 'Llandrindod Wells', 'November' and 'For the Quakers of Montgomeryshire' from *A Small Field* (1983); Nigel Jenkins: 'On the Border, Llanymynech' from *Ambush* (1966); T. Harri Jones: 'Llanafan Revisited' from *Collected Poems* (1977); Iolo Goch: 'Owain Glyndŵr's Court' from *Iolo Goch: Poems* edited and translated by Dafydd Johnston; Iorwerth Peate: 'Nant yr Eira', from *Twentieth Century Welsh Poetry* edited and translated by Joseph P. Clancy (1982); Islwyn Ffowc Elis: 'Market Day in Henberth' and 'Old Tynoro' *Cysgod y Cryman* (The Shadow of the Sickle), translated by Meic Stephens (1997).

The University of Wales Press for extracts from the following publications – Herbert Williams: *Davies the Ocean* (1992); Eirene White: *The Ladies of Gregynog* (1985); Melvin Humphreys: *The Crises of Community: Montgomeryshire* (1996); Alwyn D. Rees: *Life in a Welsh Countryside* (1951).

Macmillan Publishers Ltd for Magica Sympathia by Peter Porter published in *Max is Missing* (Picador 2001).

Hodder and Stoughton Ltd for From Llangurig to Rhayader from *Roaming Down the Wye* (1949).

Huw Jones for Long Mountain which first appeared in Poetry Wales and The Gateway to Wales from the same publication.

J.M. Dent for the extract from *Coming Down the Wye* by Robert Gibbings (1944).

Phil Carradice for In the Garden at Bronllys.

Julie Rainsbury for Powys Castle.

Norman Schweink for Gregynog Hall which first appeared in *Poetry Wales*.

David Higham Associates for a passage from *The House Under the Water* (1932) by Francis Brett Young and lines from *The Island* (1945) by the same author.

Joyce Herbert for Usk.

Dr Douglas Bassett for The Llanbrynmair Tradition.

Anthony Bailey for On Pen y Fan from *A Walk Through Wales* (Cape 1992).

The Estate of John Cowper Powys and Rod Stepney for Y Crach from *Owen Glendower* (1941).

The Estate of Harri Webb for The Village Next to Manafon.

The Estate of Hilda Vaughan for Parted from *A Thing of Nought*.

The Pathos of It from *Davies* by David Constantine (Bloodaxe 1985).

The Estate of Geraint Goodwin for Churning from *The Heyday of the Blood* (1936).

John Idris Jones for The Magic of Mr Smith from Berwin Christmas included in *Christmas in Wales* edited by Dewi Roberts (Seren 1997).

Sian James for Glyn from *And Perhaps More*.

Andrew Morrison for Border Lambing.

Peters Fraser and Dunlop for permission to reprint an extract from *Unexplained Laughter* by Alice Thomas Ellis (Duckworth 1985).

Reproduced by permission of Penguin Books Ltd Llanwddyn Submerged from *Austerlitz* by W.G. Sebald, translated by Anthea Bell (London 2001).

Reproduced by permission of Penguin Books Ltd The Last Stand of Caractacas from *The Annals of Imperial Rome* by Tacitus translated by Michael Grant.

Extract from *On the Black Hill* by Bruce Chatwin published by Jonathan Cape. Used by permission of the Random House Group Limited (1982).

Meic Stephens for A small war by Leslie Norris from *Collected Poems* (Seren).

Merryl Williams for Tretower Court.

Tony Conran for the translation of Cynddylan's Hall.

Stewart Brown and Seren for With all my griefs in my arms.

Jan Morris and Twm Morys for extracts from *A Machynlleth Triad* and *Wales: An epic view of a small country* (1992).

Graham Hartill for Cennau's Bell.

Glenda Beagan for Melangell from *Vixen* (Honno).

Siegfried Sassoon: At the grave of Henry Vaughan. Copyright Siegfried Sassoon by kind permission of George Sassoon.

Joseph P. Clancy for At the grave of Henry Vaughan.

Orion Publishing for Llanrhaeadr-ym-Mochnant from *Collected Poems* of R.S. Thomas.

Michael Joseph for The Plygain from *Guide to Traditional Customs of Britain* by Brian Shuel (1985).

Extract from *Autobiography* by Eric Gill published by Cape. Used by permission of The Random House Group Limited (1940).

Alun D. Owen for 'Reflections' from *A Montgomeryshire Youth* (Compton Books 2000).

The Estate of R.S. Thomas for 'Manafon' and 'An unanswered question' extracted from the essay 'The Paths Gone By' included in *Selected Prose* edited by Sandra Anstey (Seren).

Editor's Acknowledgements

I am indebted to Mrs Moira Dearnley for so helpfully drawing my attention to Scott's novel *The Betrothed*; Dr Ceridwen Lloyd Morgan for her information concerning Gwerful Mechain, and to Mrs Margaret Stacey, the community librarian at Newtown, for her invaluable assistance.

Topography

Magica Sympathia

Lord Herbert of Cherbury
Lounges in a thicket
Like an unpicked strawberry,
Isaac Oliver, pinxit.

Montgomery Parish Church
Keeps all the little Herberts
As terracotta dolls. Which
One is George the Wordsmith?

Magic fills the landscape –
What, here in Wales?
A flowery English handshake
For Llandrindod Wells?

Windfarm propellers' traction
Turns a Lute Book's pages,
Victorian reticulation
Laps Vyrnwy's emerald edges.

Ask the hawks which hover
Over Dinas Fawr's sheep
Who if not Glendower
Talks rivers up from creeks?

Those plush hermetic demons
Who internationalise
Wye and Lugg and Severn
Are worth a Latin phrase.

The Past is why the Present
Is packed for the Co-op.
It is and yet it isn't
That time must have a stop.

O Sympathetic Magic,
Shy fortresses and weirs!
O Forests Green and Stygic,
The wit of Passing Stairs!

Lord Herbert gave his castle
Up to Cromwell's men,
He held himself a vassal
Only to song and pen.

Peter Porter

The Eden of Wales

Central Wales may be regarded as a broad table-land, through which rivers great and small furrow their way in winding courses to the sea, but which has few clearly marked mountain ranges or stretches of fertile plain. The ancient kingdom of Powys took in most of this region, extending in its widest limits from the neighbourhood of Mold to the river Wye, near Glasbury and Hay. It included some productive districts, such as the lower valley of the Dee and the well-watered meadows of the upper Severn, so that its children were not altogether without warrant in hailing it as 'Powys, the Eden of Wales'. But most of it was pastoral upland, a country well fitted to be the nurse of a race of hardy, independent warriors, lovers of tribal freedom, haters of the sluggish and toilsome life of the lowland tiller of the soil, and tenacious holders of ancient privileges. Such were the men of Powys, inheritors of the old Brythonic traditions, in whom incessant warfare with the Mercian English kept alive the ancient tribal characteristics.

J.E. Lloyd (1861-1947): A History of Wales

From Llangurig to Rhaeader

From Llangurig to Rhaeadr there were many flower-sprinkled swards which dived down from sunlit ridges and invited me to rest my head on my knapsack, and many hidden side valleys which opened suddenly to vistas of lonely white farms and distant summits which lured me from the river banks, and many eyries and crags towards the skies which burst through great carpetings of purple heather and offered me the world if I would but climb them. Indeed it is a wonder that I ever arrived at Rhaeadr at all, there were so many inducements to turn aside and explore.

A few miles below Llangurig two hills thrust out of the moorlands and almost met to block the Wye. The narrow fields gave way to steep hanging woods whose tenacious roots were all that prevented them from sliding into the river. Knife-edged boulders, sundered and split from their parent cliffs far above, had rolled and jumped until brought suddenly to halt by tree trunks. The Wye itself was here reduced to an almost square channel, about six feet wide and nearly as deep, its bed composed of stones so coloured that the Wye assumed the tint of lime juice. A thousand feet into the sky towered grey walls of rock, their ledges decorated with delightful window-boxes of bell heather, whose purple colour splashed heedlessly upon hill and scree, and trickled down like waterfalls to form a lake of purple at the foot, which stretched for a mile distant as far as the big bend where the little River Marteg joined the Wye.

W.H. Potts: Roaming Down the Wye (1949)

Powys Paradwys Cymru

Montgomeryshire (Trefaldwyn) does not boast many tourist attractions but, to me, it is a land of marvels, marvels on a small scale; contrasted to the dramatic highlights of a European tour, they have a quiet appeal for which many may, nowadays, be grateful. Appetites are jaded: tourists are sated with spectacular monuments, great temples and theatrical landscapes; they whirl at speed through foreign countries and have no time to stay, no time in which to learn the language and to speak to the people.

Beautiful as each place may be, the traveller returns tired and often vaguely dispirited: the pace has been too hard.

It is, I think, a time in which to look at the countryside in this way. Here, in Wales, the pace is leisurely and distances are small. The English tourist has no need for a phrase-book; Welsh is spoken and is musical to listen to, but the common language is English spoken in lovely, lilting cadences. Montgomeryshire is a county of small beauties, innocent and undemanding, which, when examined minutely, are as rewarding as snowflakes under a microscope. It is a large world of small things, one of the most beautiful counties in Great Britain, *Powys Paradwys Cymru*, the Paradise of Wales.

Pauline Phillips: A View of Old Montgomeryshire (1977)

Hirnant, Powys

It didn't get a 'llan', too insignificant.
In Welsh sounds foreign, through translated
Has an ordinariness
That thorps and burys only seem to have,
Familiar on my Anglo-Saxon ear,
Their meaning now subliminal,
While this one's plain 'long stream'.

The church is later, unPevsnerian, dull,
Its vicarage now a private house –
The school too, and the indigenous
Are unmarried or unwell. Soon it will be.

An English village in the hills.
What Acts of Union, Welsh Nots couldn't crack
Falls to the trite invasion of the car.
The new ones give the required phatic wave
En route to shops that are cheaper by far,
Don't stand around in wellies discussing the weather,
Go to macramé classes or start the lingo,

Though no-one will speak it with them. What's the point?
A utilitarianism hard at first to grasp –
One with a grimness that the graveyard hints.
All the projected romance doesn't wash.

Only the rhythmn of farming still inheres
And soporofic bleating from the slopes.
The fields seen from the window
The acclivity brings improbably near.
The place is sought by those arriving with a sense
of nothing of any great consequence
Ever happening here.

Philip Carr

Climbing Towards Machynlleth

Nowadays Rayner Heppenstall is an almost forgotten figure, but in the nineteen fifties he made his mark both as a writer and as a radio producer on the BBC Third Programme.

This is Ynys-las, the tide is out. The wide estuary is all wet sand, with a narrow stream in its channel half way across. That is the Dyfi, which divides North from South Wales. Across the estuary lies Aberdovey. There is a song called 'The Bells of Aberdovey'. Blod sings it to the children, I suppose to teach them the Welsh numerals (teach me, too). It goes:

Un, dau, tri, pedwar, pump, chwech, saith,
Meddai clychau Aberdyfi . . .

The tune is without merit.

Now Glan Dyfi. The white raised letters on black, white-rimmed cast-iron glare in this disturbed sunlight, in at the window. A heron among the reeds, as we climb towards Machynlleth. Telegraph poles pass the window, not too fast but gathering speed. From right to left, they rise to the vertical and fall away. *Un, dau, tri, pedwar, pump, chwech, saith, wyth, naw . . .* A giant on stilts, hurrying to the sea, lifts one leg out of the ooze, then slaps it smartly down as he raises the other. Perhaps that unfortunate giant in the *Mabinogion* tale, not the one about Blodeuedd or Blodeuwedd, the original Flowerface, turned into an owl.

Rayner Heppenstall: 'The Woodshed' (1962)

Mellow Beauty

From the vale of Mawddwy, the Dyfi Valley opens out into a region which retains the beauty of the upper glen, but shorn of the awe and majesty which makes the isolation and grandeur of Mawddwy oppressive to the sensitive mind. This is the region of Dinas Mawddwy, Mallwyd, Cwmllinau and Cemmaes, a region not of rugged and terrible grandeur but of mellow beauty, of broad meadows and well-cultivated fields bearing crops of golden corn in their season; and the difference between Cemmaes and Mawddwy is similar to that which, as Renan has described, the traveller experiences in leaving France to enter Brittany.

About a mile below the village of Cemmaes, the river Dyfi is joined by its one important headstream-tributary, the Twymyn which flows from the wild inaccessible glens, the well-wooded slopes and the heather-covered hills of the parish of Llan bryn Mair. From the confluence the Dyfi flows in the direction of the small town of Machynlleth, below which its basin opens out to form the broad estuary which bears its name. On the northern side the yellow sands of Aber Dyfi stretch far in the direction of the Merionethshire coast; on the southern, are the beautiful woods of Glan Dyfi and the brown heathland of North Cardiganshire.

Iorwerth Peate (1901-1982):
from the Journal of the Royal Anthropological Society

A stare from the mountain

As the sun slants, the best of it over,
Into the trug of Usk from the summary
West, masking the struts, the wicker rents
With plush, with a stuff of shaded
Greens gentling the upper, thistly fields,
The thicker bush of forest, ploughland
Cuts of red already stiff in their winter
Folds, tricking the human aberration
Into the same still life, a whole
Kindred lit with the right intensity,
Painted safe to a fortunate choice
Of colours, I stand on Yscir mountain,
Head above wind level, hearing the north's
Voice at my nape, putting the frozen
Questions that the poles demand. Fieldfares
Break from a half-leaved oak as I
Walk a few tentative feet. The fetlock
Hairs, the mane, the portly grassblown
Outline of a pony natured white
Shine between me and sun, the animal
Marked with redemption from a hidden
Source. I look involuntarily, all
Of a sudden in need of a gleam
Lining my shadow. But nothing there
Satisfied, nothing anywhere in the sparse
Clip of mountain, only that down
In the valley bottom is a reed –
Plume of smoke fining the rubbish-tip –
The town, taken by sun and arked,
Burning its pages from the Domesday Book.

Roland Mathias

'A Lovely Mixture'

George Lyttelton was born at Hagley in Worcestershire and educated at Eton and Oxford. He was appointed equerry to Frederick, Prince of Wales, before entering the House of Commons at the age of twenty six as MP for Okehampton. Twenty years later he was appointed Chancellor of the Exchequer but resigned within a year. He subsequently became a baron.

We travelled with infinite pleasure (through the most charming country my eyes ever beheld, or my imagination can paint) to Powis Castle . . . It stands upon the side of a very high hill; below lies a vale of incomparable beauty, with the Severn winding through it, the town of Welsh-Pool, terminated with high mountains. The opposite side is beautifully cultivated half way up, and green to the top, except in one or two hills, whole summits are rocky, and of grotesque shapes, that give variety and spirit to the prospect. Above the castle is a long ridge of hills finely shaded, part of which is the park, and still higher is a terrace, up to which you are led through very fine lawns, from whence you have a view that exceeds all description. The county of Montgomery, which lies all within this view, is to my eyes the most beautiful in South Britain; and though I have not been in Scotland, I cannot believe I shall find any place there superior, or equal, to it; because the highlands are all uncultivated, and the lowlands want wood; whereas this country is admirably shaded with hedge-rows. It has a lovely mixture of corn-fields and meadows, though more of the latter. The vales and bottoms are large, and the mountains, that rise like a rampart all around, add a magnificence and grandeur to the scene, without giving you any horror or dreadful ideas, because at Powis Castle they appear at such a distance as not to destroy the beauty and softness of the country between them.

George Lyttelton (1709-1773): An Account of a Journey into Wales

'A Good Fashionable Place'

In passing Montgomery-shire, we were so tired with rocks and mountains, that we wish'd heartily we had kept close to the sea shore, but it not much mended the matter if we had, as I understood afterwards: The River Severn is the only beauty of this county, which rising I say, out of the Plymlymon Mountain, receives instantly so many other rivers into its bosom, that it becomes navigable before it gets out of the county; namely, at Welch Pool, on the edge of Shropshire. This is a good fashionable place, and has many English dwelling in it, and some very good families; but we saw nothing farther worth remarking.

The vales and meadows upon the bank of the Severn, are the best of this county, I had almost said, the only good part of it; some are of opinion, that, the very water of the Severn, like that of Nile, impregnates the valleys, and when it over-flows, leaves a vertue behind it, particularly to itself; and this they say is confirm'd, because all the country is so fruitful, wherever this river does overflow, and its waters reach. The town, or rather as the natives call it, the city of Montgomery, lyes not far from this river, on the outer edge of the country next to Herefordshire. This was, it seems, a great frontier town in the wars between the English and the Welch, and was beautify'd and fortify'd by King Henry III; the town is now much decay'd: It gives title to the eldest son of the ducal house of Powis, who is call'd Lord Montgomery, and Marquis of Powis; they have a noble seat at Troy, hard by this town on the other side the river: But the house of Pembroke also claims the title of Montgomery.

This county is noted for an excellent breed of Welch horses, which, though not very large, are exceeding valuable, and much esteem'd all over England; all the North and West part of the county is mountainous and stony. We saw a great many old monuments in this country, and Roman camps wherever we came, and especially if we met any person curious in such things, we found they had many Roman coins.

Daniel Defoe (1660-1731):
A Tour Through the Whole Island of Great Britain

'The Grand Cataract'

There are many remarkable cataracts in Britain and the neighbouring isles, even the little Celtic Isle of Man has its remarkable waterfall; but this Rhaeadr, the grand cataract of North Wales, far exceeds them all in altitude and beauty, though it is inferior to several of them in the volume of its flood. I never saw water falling so gracefully, so much like thin beautiful threads as here. Yet even this cataract has its blemish. What beautiful object has not something which more or less mars its loveliness? There is an ugly black bridge or semi-circle of rock, about two feet in diameter and about twenty feet high, which rises some little way below it, and under which the water, after reaching the bottom passes, which intercepts the sight, and prevents it from taking in the whole fall at once. This unsightly object has stood where it now stands since the day of creation and will probably remain there to the day of judgment. It would be a desecration of nature to remove it by art, but no one could regret if nature in one of her floods were to sweep it away.

George Borrow (1803-1881): Wild Wales

Debatable Land

Robert Roberts, Y Sgolor Mawr [The Great Scholar] was born near Llangernyw, a village in what is now the county of Conwy. He was ordained as an Anglican priest in 1860, but decided to leave the church. He then emigrated to Australia where he wrote his fascinating autobiography. In 1875 he returned to Wales and was employed as a private tutor. Here we find him at Castle Caereinion.

It was situated in a pleasant glen, fertile and well-wooded, opening out into the great valley of the Severn. Offa's Dyke could be traced a mile or two to the east-ward, and the line of demarcation between English and Welsh ran through the parish. The lower division was entirely English, and the upper Welsh, while the village situated about the centre was a sort of Debatable Land. Both languages were known pretty generally, especially by the elder folk, though English was mostly spoken: as to the children, they used English exclusively. And in external features also the country partook of the characteristics of both countries: on the one hand we had a rich, fat valley, thoroughly English in its look of abundance and comfort; on the other, there was a Welsh succession of hills and dales, less rich but very pleasing to look at. On the English side the houses were mostly of brick, red, square, and rather ugly, but the huge ricks, sleek cattle, and blooming orchards took off much of the barrenness. In the Welsh division the houses were built in that most picturesque of styles, with frames of oak, the interstices being filled up with lath and plaster. The poorest thatched cottage had its garden, well filled with fruit trees; the poverty that the richest land is not totally exempt from, was well hidden beneath a mask of picturesqueness, and one might well forget for a time that it had any existence. Coming as I did from a part of the country very uninviting to the eye, the beauty of Castle Caereinion was more striking than it would have been to one familiar with a richer landscape: to me it had all the beauty of Carmel and Sharon combined.

Robert Roberts (1834-1885):
The Life and Opinions of a Wandering Scholar

A Pioneering Study

First published in 1950, when little had hitherto been written on the social organisation of rural communities in Britain, Alwyn D. Rees' Life in a Welsh Countryside *has attained the status of a classic and as such it has had considerable influence of subsequent works exploring the life of other communities. It describes and analyses the culture of rural Wales as it manifested itself over half a century ago in a parish in northern Montgomeryshire.*

The civil parish of Llanfihangel yng Ngwynfa covers about fifteen-and-a-half square miles of upland country in northern Montgomeryshire. To the north and west of it are the high moorlands of the Berwyn, while south-eastwards the land falls towards the Vyrnwy and Severn valleys and the Shropshire Plain beyond. The scenery is typical of much of the Welsh uplands, with round-topped hills forming a gently undulating skyline broken here and there by a rocky summit. Between the hills, through deep steep-sided valleys, run the little tributaries draining the area into the River Vyrnwy which forms the southern boundary of the parish. Most of the hills in the northern half of the parish are over 1,000 feet, and the boundary deviates for a short distance to follow a ridge above 1,400 feet. The south is generally lower, the hills seldom reach the 1,000 foot line while the floor of the Vyrnwy valley falls below 600 feet. Rough grass, bracken and a little gorse form the natural vegetation of the hill-tops, and there is a little bog-land in some of the hollows of the north. The woods on the steeper slopes and along the banks of streams remind us of the forests that filled the valleys in olden times. But as one moves northwards across the parish the trees become fewer and the moorlands more continuous.

Nine-tenths of the inhabitants live in scattered farms and cottages, a few of which stand along the road-sides while the majority are well back among the fields and are connected with the roads and with each other by a network of rough tracks and footpaths.

Alwyn D. Rees (1911-1974): Life in a Welsh Countryside

The Gateway to Wales

In the late fifties we lived in Birmingham where my father taught history. My memories are faded pictures of catching buses home from the city; Mam coming home from hospital with a baby sister; learning to read with Dick, Dora, Nip and Fluff.

We moved to Welshpool in 1961. I crossed Broad Street each morning, glanced up at the Town Hall clock and hurried along to Berriew Road Junior School, satchel bouncing on my back. For two first language pupils in our class, Welsh lessons were in the Headmaster's study. Under a high Victorian window and behind a large wooden table, I sat entranced by the Headmaster's dramatic renderings of Pwyll and Pryderi's adventures to strange lands.

Welshpool is an anglicised market town often referred to as the Gateway to Wales. In the Dream of Rhonabwy, one of seven other tales of the *Mabinogion*, Arthur and his knights were to be seen encamped along the river Severn near Welshpool, probably the battle at nearby Buttington in 893. Henry Tudor is also reputed to have camped outside Welshpool on his way to the Battle of Bosworth in 1485. Every summer we were invaded by queues of cars and caravans heading for the coast from the Midlands. Most winters after snow and heavy rain we were besieged by the river, cut-off by road as the brown flood-water plundered low-lying farms and houses.

Across the valley stood Long Mountain, a green ridge that looked down on the town like those watchers in the iron-age hill fort of Beacon Ring or those on Offa's Dyke which crosses the high lonely skyline. Most mornings as I walked down to the High School it would catch my eye, its familiar pattern of fields and woods brooding under cloud or beaming in early sun, mist lingering along the valley and the school's playing fields.

Huw Jones in an article in 'Poetry Wales' (1997)

Manafon

One lives according to the seasons there, and of course there is more variation than the sea. The winters were pretty hard in Manafon. If there was snow about, we were sure to get it. In the bad winter of 1947, our lane was blocked with snow from the house to the main road and we were unable to use the car for nine weeks. Some nights there would be a bitter frost too, and one night that winter we had forty-two degrees of frost. I can remember hearing the house cracking as the ice took hold of it, and by the morning it was impossible to see through the window so thick were the fronds of ice. Oh, how we welcomed the spring after such a winter, the first buds on the trees, the trout back in their old haunts in the bright river.

And then after a long, hot summer, the leaves would start to change colour, and for two months the valley would be like fairyland: the cherry-trees dark red, and the ash-trees yellow. There was a large ash-tree at the end of the Rectory lane which would be completely yellow by November. The leaves remained on it one autumn longer than usual. But there was heavy frost one night and the next day as the sun rose, the leaves began to fall. They went on falling for hours making the tree like a golden fountain playing silently in the sun; I shall never forget it.

And when the autumn came, the foxes would start to bark and the men would go after them. It was a strange kind of hunting that went on in the Manafon district. No horses of course, the land was too mountainous. No, they hunted on foot until they lost the trail and the dogs, and then wandered about for hours in the twilight. I often heard the sound of the horn high on the hillsides about nine at night, as the hunters searched for their dogs. There was something very odd about it, as though the 'little people' were hunting for make-believe foxes in the clouds. But what a place for owls! On a quiet night with a full moon, the valley rang with the sound of the owls, as though they had all come to hold an *eisteddfod* . . .

R.S. Thomas (1913-2000):
Selected Prose, edited by Sandra Anstey

'Damn English!'

. . . I could easily be in a completely English village in the heart of England. The accent you'll hear on the street or in the shop isn't at all Welsh. The colourless English of small gentlemen farmers and wives of military officers or deputy managers of Gwent and Glamorgan's factories and business offices who have settled in an agreeable spot within easy reach of their work, that's what's most prominent, mixed perhaps with the voices of the pony trekkers who support what is one of this region's chief industries now, at least in summer. Indeed at times the town seems to be full of long-faced horsey women! Perhaps I'm mistaken, too, about the Englishness of Crickhowell (Crucywel). There are, after all, many different kinds of Welsh men and women, and thank goodness for the variety. I well remember being vastly surprised once in the bar of Gwesty'r Arth by hearing a remarkably English voice complaining terribly about some wrong its owner had suffered at the hand of the 'damn English'!

Alun Llewelyn-Williams (1913-1988): The Light in the Gloom,
translated by Joseph P. Clancy

Crickhowel

C rowded with beauties in thy lovely vale,
R ich scenes and varied meet the wanderer's eye;
I n green-leaved groves the cushat tells its tale,   *(wood-pigeon)*
C ooing a love-song to its mate close by:
K ept spellbound have our wandering footsteps been
H ere by Porthmawr, while we enchanted gazed
O n the luxuriant splendour of that scene
W here, winding down the dale, Usk's waters blazed
E ffulgent in the sun, like molten gold;
L ingered we there till evening mists across the landscape rolled.

Richard Hall (1817-1866)

Llanthony

In 1807 the ruined Augustinian priory at Llanthony was purchased by Walter Savage Landor who planned to develop the extensive grounds and live the life of a member of the squirearchy. He was refused permission to restore the priory but lived in a habitable wing of the large building. In 1811 he married Julia Thuïllier and they frequently entertained prominent guests, including Southey. But Landor possessed a cantankerous streak and soon quarrelled with his neighbours. The remainder of his stay in the area was short lived.

I

Llanthony! an ungenial clime,
And the broad wing of restless Time,
Have rudely swept thy massy walls
And rockt thy abbots in their palls.
I loved thee by the streams of yore,
By distant streams I love thee more;
For never is the heart so true
As bidding what we love adieu.

II

Along Llanthony's ruin'd aisles we walk'd
And woods then pathless, over verdant hill

And ruddy mountain, and aside the stream
Of sparkling Honddu. Just at close of day
There by the comet's light we saw the fox
Rush from the alders, nor relax in speed
Until he trod the pathway of his sires
Under the hoary crag of Comioy.

Walter Savage Landor (1775-1864)

Plynlimon (Pumlumon)

The first time that I heard the second symphony of Sibelius was after I had spent a night on Plynlimon. It seemed, as I listened, that I was back again on those hills, and that every emotion I had experienced there was now clarified and accentuated. In the opening chords I could sense the calm of evening, with dusk creeping into the valleys; an ominous calm, for dark clouds were banking over the distant hills. There was the cry of birds, and wind singing through the heather. Clouds piling overhead were mirrored in a peaty pool.

Rain began to fall. Big drops. Bigger drops. Bubbles on the water. Wind and more wind. A deluge of rain. All sounds drowned by the rumbling of the thunder.

A vivid afterglow. Velvet darkness.

Then in the second movement that marvellous plucking of the strings. Sleep. Sleep. Sleep. Deep heavy sleep, undisturbed by passing squalls or spattering of rain. Sleep.

And after the first glow of dawn wild streaks of light shooting up behind ragged clouds. There is a surge and swell of waking life. It is fantasy, of course, but in those tender passages which follow I perceived a human element. A sprite maybe; laughing, leaping, splashing through the soggy bogs. She calls, and together we race from ridge to ridge, from combe to combe, through sun and shower until we find the lake that is at the head of the stream.

Then the music swells with triumph, and a peace that passes all understanding pervades the hill-side. In the fourth movement the triumph heightens. Harmony upon harmony, and exultant peace of mind. Grandeur piles upon grandeur, crescendo upon crescendo, of joy, and glory, and praise.

Robert Gibbings: Coming Down the Wye (1942)

31

At Llyn Clywedog

You need to use imagination
To see it now as they did then.
Monuments soon revert to stones,
Deep reservoirs to sea-green pools,
And no man walking on the shore
Hears, far down, a tolling bell,
Or suspects it there. Today, a buzzard
Circled Pen y Gaer, its prey
Trapped somewhere between the icy
Water and the peak. We sat in the car
And watched it from the Viewing Point,
No more than ordinary tourists
Except for the time of year, the snow,
The picnic tables turned for once,
And our eyes, averted from the water.
Did we choose to come here, then,
To make amends? Because we must?
                              Where we live,
Tryweryn, Clywedog, Claerwen, Fyrnwy,
Were never more than distant names.
Were never the sign they took them for:
Like lichen patterned on a rock,
The irredeemable stain. I have a liking
For moving water, not still like this,
And the image of those buttresses
Hollow, massive, 'like cathedral vaults',
I would not choose. For this is a place
You visit when the sun is shining,
Dispelling the eerie silence of it,
The flat and depthless calm. And best leave
Strictly by the road you came,
The one with No Exit painted on it.

Graham Thomas

Forest Fawr

Francis Brett Young enjoyed a wide readership during his lifetime, although his fictional output is variable in terms of quality. Certain episodes of some of his novels were set in mid Wales but one of his best known works The House Under the Water *is the only one to be set entirely within the region. Many years ago it was adapted for television.*

The mass of mountains called Forest Fawr sprawls over the middle March of Wales like a carved lion crouched in defiance. From a distance of fifty miles and more that huge shade dominates the border landscape. At its northern extremity two moulded domes, one behind and surmounting the other, resemble a silhouette of gigantic loins from which a line of escarpment, running due south in the likeness of falling flanks and a level backbone, rises proudly, abruptly, at last into contours of shoulder and neck, maned with streaks of naked stone (for no living wood can survive the rigours of such uplifting), and a massive head gazing eastward over the dwarfed hills of Radnor. Below flows a turbulent river which one stony paw, protruded from a chest shagged with forest, has thrust out of its natural course, purloining, by the same gesture, some thousands of acres of man's pasturage that lie crushed beneath it like a lion's kill, a token and a warning of the monster's negligent strength.

All evil proceeds from the Forest. The Romans knew it – those iron men who took the Alps in their stride. Their story is scored on the land in roads like sword-cuts. From Wroxeter, by Severn, the white city that the Saxon burnt, they set out boldly. There is a military post near Lesswardine on the banks of Teme. Still westward they marched, and the road reeled out behind them till the lion of Forest Fawr rose up in their path. At this point something happened. None will ever know what it was. Sudden panic; the smell of failure; invincible promptings of caution . . . They doubted and turned in their tracks. The road shadows forth the tale. First it falters and serves, as though turned from its purpose by some force of nature. Then, pricked by indomitable will, it is thrown forward a league, to end on the verge of a sudden hill-crest like a broken aqueduct. On the eastern side of the hill a square earthwork remains. The superstitious avoid it; they say it is haunted, though by what none can tell. Broad-leaved, virulent nettles possess it, and two black yews, whose roots and the scrabbling claws of the badger have brought to light triangular shards of fire-blackened Samian and three coins of small value – one of Constantine, and two of Severus, minted at York. That is all, and enough.

So the light of Rome faded and Wroxeter roared up in flame. Yet the folk who dragged their wains over the road the Roman had left and still hold the lands he abandoned have no less fear of Forest Fawr. Though the mountain put on its most gentle disguises and smile on them they are not beguiled. When its substance, dissolving, resembles on opaline cloud; when its smooth flanks are dappled with shadows of cumulus; when wet rocks are mica, and blowing bracken a sheen of bronze, they still shake their heads. 'The old mountain,' they say, 'do be looking too peart this evening.' In vain does the monster trail its silvery lambskins! They know its true habit of stark and inky sable; and if they love it no better they trust it no less in its proper colour. They are Saxon folk, born of woodlands and bred to the plough. The river is their frontier; beyond it dwell mystery and evil, in a wilderness peopled by a dark and dwarfish race; men quick-witted for bargaining, with a secret speech of their own, false-smiling and ruthless; fatal women, long-limbed, with milk-white skins and red hair, frail, seductive and slovenly. Wise men beware and have small truck with either. For no good can come out of the mountain.

Francis Brett Young (1884-1954): 'The House Under the Water'

In the Garden at Bronllys

(Two poems)

I

Sun drowned blackbirds
dart July,
cut through the day
like knives
in melted butter.

But we, grown languid,
visionary eyed,
dream opiate dreams,
remain untouched
by everything
but sun.

II

Purple Emperors in tree tops,
simple moments in the sun.
Afternoons when heat
lies fragile as a poem
and only momentary wings
disturb the torpor of the day.

Silently we dream –

disquieting impressions,
moments strangely sad
beneath the flare and fanfare
of intransigent
butterfly wings.

Phil Carradice

Llandrindod Wells,
November

November crawls back
to a masked disco,
grins through the hotel window
face seared with flame.

Wind rifles hedgerows
matted with mist,
        ribs protruding
through torn uniform.

Rockets whistle
stars abandon their posts,
        ragged ghosts
vanish on burning ships.

Crowds on the quayside cheer,
children shoulder-high
shriek and wave sparklers
in the school playground

In the museum gardens
a blackbird's bugle fades,
the cenotaph's initialled bark
banked with fallen blossom.

In a cold terraced kitchen
the kettle boils dry
        Widowed, she stares
through a cove of smoke.

Huw Jones

On Hay Bridge

8.00 pm in a belated spring
in still air under marbled sky
trees stand foot to foot on their reflections.
The river dimpling only over stones
goes glassy at its edge,
is clear beneath me.

A salmon a yard long, dark slate
blotched with sour milk,
twitches against the flow,
sways, mirroring the ropes of weed,
sidewinds, sideslips, tacks upstream.
Gerallt saw her eight hundred journeys back.

The banks no doubt were greengorged then in spring.
In clearings spent homesteads smouldered.
Wooden towers, slowly, were rebuilt in stone.
Castles studded conquerors' intent,
stitched the sleeve with rock.
Lords dead in Gwent. A headless corpse in Cwm Hir.

Three hundred years of gradual collapse
and Bedo Brwynllys near here
sang sweet and politic of loving girls
and how their eyebrows curved
like rainbows or like squirrels' tails.
Namesake, let me not be you.

Eight hundred years and still we say
you lose less by retreat.
Some martyred hero and a moving song
will do to warm an evening perhaps.
In daylight, let the current inch you back
against yourself.

The light, waning, cools mirrored greens
to lave thought, blooms the river with
a promise of opacity. Swallows,

openthroated, trawl the air for flies
beneath the bridge, drive on like the salmon
and let their element wash thorough.

She, slatemilk, edging out of sight
slides under the reflected trees.
Come back, I think. Come rain
to puncture all reflection.
Give me that pied yard of muscle
to inch against what pushes me from home.

Christopher Meredith

Powis Castle

Moated in the deer park,
Italian terraces still hang here,
drip above a more fashionable
wilderness. Only ferns, ivy

now swirl the cool eddies
of an Orangery washed
by fuchsia, purple-monkshood,
a spray of tea-scented rose.

Baroque pleasure pools have gone,
but urns jut as breakwaters
into this raised tide of flowers.
Box and yew billow paths, tumble

down to rill the formal garden
where avenues of apple and vine
buoy towards a dry fountain,
float in gilded marjoram.

Julie Rainsbury

The Road to Montgomery (Trefaldwyn)

O revengeful gods, have you condemned me to tramp along this hellish road for ever, have you removed Montgomery with a thunderbolt so that there is nothing at the other end of this road, no inn, no bed, no supper, no beer? O just and compassionate gods, have pity upon my feet!

What a road! It ran straight between dull hedgerows. Small and uninviting hills rose on each side of it. Not even a beetle stirred on its smooth hard surface. It was a geometrically straight line, I thought, having no beginning and no end. (If there is a Hell for Hikers, such roads will surely exist there.)

I wondered wretchedly what sort of a place Montgomery was, since the road which led to it was so deserted. No one came from Montgomery; no one – save my foolish young self – was optimistic enough to go to Montgomery. Perhaps there was no such place. Perhaps Montgomery was a myth, having no existence in fact, but merely a spurious sort of existence on maps and in guide-books.

John Moore (1907-1967): The Welsh Marches

Gregynog Hall

I wonder whether ghosts of the dead sisters
still roam these corridors, exasperated,
wishing they had it all back, and vaguely
searching the bedrooms for an honest man.
No spectral sightings yet have been reported,
no clankings, groans, mysterious moving objects,
no morbid smells nor columns of cold air,
and yet I feel strong presences in this house,
ghosts of my own: they disappear round corners,
their voices echo in the cobbled courtyard,
they look up smiling from a chair and vanish.
It's wrong to meet or mate with ghosts, I know.
It's cruel and sad to keep the dead alive,
but harder than ever now to let them die.

Norman Schwenk

Llanafan Unrevisited

I took for emblem the upland moors and the rocky
Slopes above them, bitter parishes
Of the buzzard striking from lonely circles
And the ragged fox hunting the lean
Rabbits, and the starved preacher nourishing
A little heat from a hell that once had meaning.
I had thought to be a proud man and isolated,
Inviolate as my hills even in defeat,
Not easily marked even by the incessant
Savagery of weather, God, and my relations.
Small, maybe, but tough I thought and unendearing
As feg and able to endure weather
That smashes the great oaks and makes mud
Of the good meadows and destroys good men.

And now I live in the good meadows, and I have
No emblem except your body, and I am
Still a member of a narrow chapel, and a boy
From a hungry parish, a spoiled preacher,
Greedily taking the surplus of your sunshine,
And still afraid of hell because I've been there.

T. Harri Jones (1921-1965)

The River

The silver Severn water
It winds its way at ease
Across the amber pebbles,
Beneath the alder trees,
And all day long its quiet voice
Is sweet to me as my heart's choice.

The dark pool holds the otter;
We hunted him at morn
When dewy, airy gossamers
Were hung on every thorn,
But though we saw his silver chain
Till noon we holloaed there in vain.

Then when the orchard grasses
Were flecked with shade and sun,
Barefooted to the water
We boys and girls would run,
And leaping there would plunge and swim
Through broken lights and shadows dim.

Ah, where are now the voices
That echoed on those shores?
And where the jolly boatmen
Who dipped their yellow oars?
The sunset lingers in the sky,
But still the changing stream runs by.

Eiluned Lewis (1900-1979)

The Teme

So, with alternate gloom and shine,
Teme falls by Llanfairwaterdine
To Knucklas village and Knighton Vale,
Where the felled woods lie silver-pale
With floss of silken willow-weed;
And on her face the windblown seed
Lighteth softer than thistledown
To drift and skim, like mayflies blown
To their death in June – till a tiny waft
Of light air lifteth it aloft,
And the seed goes sailing on its way,
While sweet Teme floweth without stay
Between the wild flags' clustered swords,
Where gentle, wide-horned Herefords
Bend their white-muzzled heads to drink
From muddy pools on the trampled brink;
Or stand knee-deep in the cool stream
In an unimaginable dream
And slowly swing their tails, while flies
Settle on their uncurious eyes;
Till the roofs of a rising village strown
On a steep hillside, and a tower of stone,
Stand in her path and halt her flow,
And clear Teme feels the undertow
Of denser waters that have run
From the marly dales of Corve and Clun,
And the streams of the confluent rivers mingle
In a deep pool that laps the shingle
Where the twin sisters meet and twine
Under the bridge at Leintwardine
And the two waters flow as one . . .

Francis Brett Young (1884-1954): The Island

Little of Distinction

Little of distinction, guide-books had said –
a marshy common and a windy hill:
a renovated church, a few old graves
with curly stones and cherubs with blind eyes:
yews with split trunks straining at rusty bands:
and past the church, a house or two, a farm,
not picturesque, not even very old.
And yet, the day I went there, life that breaks
so many promises gave me a present
it had not promised – I found this place
had beauty after all. How could I have seen
how a verandah's fantastic curlicues
would throw a patterned shadow on the grass?
or thought how delicate ash-leaves would stir
against a sky of that young blue? or known
trees and grey walls would have such truthful beauty,
like and exact statement? And least of all
could I have foreseen the miles on hazy miles
of Radnorshire and Breconshire below,
uncertain in the heat – the mystery
that complements precision. So much sweeter
was this day than the expectation of it.

                                        Ruth Bidgood

Sheep on the Brecon hills

Salmon
       Swim over ancient cobbles,
Mirror dancing through mirror,
                                Sheep
On the Brecon hills
    Framed between chimney pots
Of the town,
       Each fragrance
With the smell of cut grass;
          In holiday jobs
Teenage schoolgirls
    Abhor wearing National costume.

The Market clock
          Stopped for over a century
       Displays
An Out of Order notice
    For the tourists,
          Roses around the door
Of a firm of solicitors,

                         A butterfly
With quarrelling wings.

       On half-drowned banks
Of a carpeted pool
    Picnickers
       Beneath a birch
As if silvered
       Only by the wind.

                         Gloria Evans Davies

44

Usk

That river rumbles in my memory still,
Muscular, galloping down its bed in spate,
Even in a dry June hurrying.
Pools deep as pits, greenbrown glass lapping
Flat stones, but trenched suddenly, riven,
Sly for the awkward foot.
Bats fished it at dusk, dipping for flyhatches,
Little drunken black bunches of leaves diving, sidling.
Dabchicks and otters wrinkled the surface.
At night you heard the length of the river grinding,
Tooling the stone sides sullenly, there were
Splashes, whistling calls, bullocks tearing the grass,

And above the Maiden's Pool
A presence softly clinging to the air,
A shiver of light, mournful and young.
I see myself dreaming across the stiles,
Creeping the dangerous places
Where there were no handholes and a slip
Meant the brown water overhead.
I remember the Usk for its treachery,
Its shadow upon joy. It was as dangerous
As I was, then.

Joyce Herbert

By Bronllys Castle

And this, perhaps, is where I find my place
In all that web of routes and possibilities:
Tending my safe and ordered garden
By the new home; planning walks with maps
Across a man-soaked countryside;
Feeling the hill, the stream, the fortress
Ring perfect in the picture's harmony.

Strange then that I caught this tower – mostly
Gothic for strolling tourists after tea –
In hard dusk grey and aching in the wind
The mountains rolling up a dead wave and
A remote bird flapping dark against a cloud.
Easy to picture in the pinched ogee
The predatory eye of some cool thug
Asserting lordship from his dead tower.
And the copper beech clutching its black flakes
Tossed and surged against the stone.

I walked down to the river's edge,
Became warm, slithered over mud, was afraid
To touch the long grasses lush after
Sun and spate, forced through choking nettles
Laced across with campion and saw in the
Submarine light of stalks huge dock leaves turned
A sick white-green. In an arrow of late sun
Wild rhubarb immense by the river nodded
A fandance, a come-on across the water
Stems bending under poison canopies;
And failing to find the path that should be there
I slid drowning through weeds into a fence.
There was a dull explosion in the gloom
And I saw, above, the cool predator,
That flat-faced bird that burst from the tree
Shattering the flakes on the living tower
Throbbing like a bomb on pulsing wings,
Beneath my heel, the claw-print in the mud.

                                        Christopher Meredith

Night on the Dyke

Night falls on the Dyke
    like a sigh.
and the trees lean towards the horizon.

The clouds of twilight press
    like steel soles
on the nape of the oak,
and the arms of the elm are slack
in the chains of the gloom.
Naked is the flesh of the ash
    to the bites of the bayonets of the darkness,
and the maple kneels
    under the lash of the north wind.

The Dyke has been conquered tonight,
and the scream of branches
freezes the air
under the torture
    of the imperialism of night.

Bryan Martin Davies, translated by Grahame Davies

Llanfihangel

Some still remember the rose-window
shining through dusk, the bells
that played hymn-tunes, the one
that tolled for the valley's dead.
Splendid Victorian folly, the church itself
lived less than a century. Soft stone
sopped up the endless rain. Above cross-point
of nave and transept, heavy tower
made an infinitesimal shift, chancel arch
moved a millimetre out of true.
In the pulpit, an intermittent drip
punctuated sermons. Whisper by whisper
flaking began, softest of plaster-fall
from pillar and wall, drift of dust
on chaliced wine. Then as a doomed mind,
whose tiny eccentricities have given
little unease, suddenly lurches to grosser
irrationality, the building shed
a first sodden chunk of facing-stone,
and was put away.
Damp barricaded silence lasted
till the slow thudding months of demolition,
the final blasting of the tower.
Grass, yew-trees, graves remain,
and in a few old minds regret
no longer sharp, but steady as rain
that brought down stone and fed the flood of grass.

Ruth Bidgood

The Llanbryn-Mair Tradition

The Llanbryn-Mair tradition: why make such a statement at all? Some of you know that I was trained in the Aberystwyth College's School of Geography and it is natural for me, therefore, to search for some of the basic reasons for this area's distinctive features. It is a land safe on the western side of Talerddig pass. Beyond that pass over the centuries, wave after wave of foreign influences have surged from the east, with this land behind the pass. Many of these influences were not at all harmful. As Belloc once said, any community which lives in total isolation will surely wither, but the community that is surrounded by solid natural defences, and yet has a doorway to receive new influences and ideas and the ability to assimilate them in its life, is bound to develop an independent mind. Such was Llanbryn-Mair on the western side of Talerddig pass, aware of all the dangers of the constant surge from the east.

How many of you, at some time, have stood on the ruins of Owain Cyfeiliog's castle at Tafolwern? That's the place for you to gain an understanding of the background to Llanbryn-Mair's tradition. When you stand there with the rivers Iaen and Twymyn in a loop around you, you can see the parish's low ground, from Mynydd Rhiwsaeson to Creigiau Pennant, reaching on either side of you and straight in front of you, Talerddig pass opening like a door to the unexpected. And behind the door, in one row, are Diosg, Hafod-y-bant, Tŷ Mawr and Tafolwern castle. If you were to ask me for a picture of what is meant by this tradition, this is what I would offer you; that small castle during the turbulent early period of the Middle Ages defending the independence of Cyfeiliog and in later years, when Wales's character had strengthened, Tŷ Mawr and Diosg defending the independent mind and spirit of the Welshman, and between them Hafod-y-bant, the home of the meek and mild saint, Richard Tibbott, representing the gentleness and tolerance that develop when one establishes a living in this tradition.

Douglas A. Bassett: from the text of a lecture delivered to the Honourable Society of Cymmrodorion, 1954.

On Pen-y-Fan

It was two fifty-five pm when I reached the flat summit of Pen-y-Fan. The other party of hikers – two men and two women in serious climbing kit – were already there. It struck me that for most of the day I'd been absolutely on my own and here, on the highest, toughest ground, I was in company. Perhaps those who had worries about possible overuse of a Cambrian Way, taking in all these peaks, had grounds for their concern. In any event, if those of us up there had come for the view, the weather suddenly obliged. On really clear days, so it is said, you can see all the way to Plynlimon, a mountain some forty miles north of here. Now, although nothing like that was possible, the clouds had parted. A hazy sun shone. To the south I had a view over the reservoirs almost to Merthyr. The upper faces of the mountain resembled old light-green velvet, very thin and worn. On the north and east sides Pen-y-Fan fell away in almost sheer drops. I stood for a few minutes a little way back from the north edge, rocking slightly from the strength of the wind that hit the scarp and came over the top. In *The Mabinogion*, Arthur's knights Kay and Bedevere sat on top of Plynlimon 'in the highest wind in the world'. This wind also felt high, but, as in a sailing boat or open plane, it made you feel as if you were in motion. The air, the wind, was blowing solidly toward Pen-y-Fan, and the earth, the mountain, the summit of Pen-y-Fan, was turning through the wind.

The pleasure of reaching the top of a mountain is not long-lasting. Like other pleasures, it is soon followed by thoughts of what comes next, in this case descent. I went down westwards, along the back of Pen-y-Fan's slightly lower sister, Corn Du; then over a ridge and northwestward to where the steep scarp rises above a small finger bowl of a lake, Llyn Cwm Llwch. Here stood a rough stone obelisk with an inscription: THIS OBELISK MARKS THE SPOT WHERE THE BODY OF TOMMY JONES AGED 5 WAS FOUND. HE LOST HIS WAY BETWEEN CWMLLWCH FARM AND THE LOGIN ON THE NIGHT OF AUGUST 4TH 1900. AFTER AN ANXIOUS SEARCH OF 29 DAYS HIS REMAINS WERE DISCOVERED SEPT 2. ERECTED BY VOLUNTARY SUBSCRIPTIONS. W. POWELL PRICE, MAYOR OF BRECON 1901.

Anthony Bailey: A Walk Through Wales (1992)

People

'Y Crach'

John Cowper Powys' novel Owen Glendower *is set in various places within Wales and England between 1400 and 1416. It has been claimed that in his portrayal of Owen, Cowper Powys was projecting aspects of his own psychology. In the early pages we encounter a vividly realised character from Llanfechain.*

With less trepidation than many young men would have felt – but his nearness to his ancestral fortress seemed a stronger armour than any that Griffin could carry – Rhisiart boldly advanced to the agitated group of persons who were arguing and disputing at the brink of the ford.

Two dismounted riders, leading their horses, approached him at once, and one of them, greeting him in a pleasant manner by name, introduced him to the other.

'He gave me the slip, this young gentleman,' he remarked in English with an indulgent smile. 'Rhisiart ab Owen his name is, if I get it right; but yours, Master, if you'll pardon me for saying so, hardly seems . . . '

'Seems or not seems, Master Brut,' cried the Lollard's companion, 'the young gentleman will have to call me what all Powys and Yale and Cynllaith Owen and Glyndyfrdwy and Maelor and Bromfield and Chirk-land call me, or he may call me King of the Fornicators. "Y Crach", the Scab, is my name, born in Ffinnant near little Llanfechain, where every maid is my cousin and every old trot my god-mother! No, you needn't blush to look at 'em, young master. Birth-marks all, birth-marks all! And by whom were they put on me, think ye? Every jack one of them, by Holy Derfel, when I came out of Sister's belly! Sister Mallt she was, my blessed mother, God give her peace; and "Y Crach", of Ffinnant near Llanfechain, I am, young master! Every man born knows Llanfechain where the great hanging oak is, and where Sheriff Burnell's grandmother, he who now's so hot for the new King, were drowned in green pond for a whore of Satan. And there's no Welshman, nor no Englishman neither, between Chester and Chirk that doesn't know "Y Crach", the Scab. Listen to me, young gentleman,' and to Rhisiart's disgust the fellow laid a hand on his black sleeve. 'How do I manage it, so as to have no enemy in all the Marches? Is that what you're asking? Well!' and he lowered his voice, 'I'll tell you! 'Tis these here rose-petals as does it,' and with a wicked grimace he tapped his shocking facial disfigurement, which certainly had the effect of intensifying the halcyon blue colour of his one remaining eye to such a point that Rhisiart found it hard to keep his eyes away from it. 'But that's not all', and the Scab proceeded to close this bright window to his roguish soul with a cyclopean wink. 'First and last, 'tis all Holy Derfel's work. He put these rosy-posies on me afore I came out of my poor mother; and do 'ee know who *her* were? Her were a dedicated nun; and to bear a *baban* to Derfel were too much for the maid. They didn't have to do nothing to her. She died in peace. She died smiling and whispering to her *baban* and calling on Derfel. That's who she called on, young man, Blessed Saint Derfel; and seeing you're a friend of Master Brut here, who's the best Christian poor old Scab have met for many a year, I thought it best to tell you who I were and who, in a manner of speaking, me parents were, so that there'd be no mistake. Presently if, as I hope God wills, we'll pass the night together I'll compose a poem for you. I've already composed five for Master Brut; and if he writes them down later, as he says he's a mind to, maybe he'll do the same for yours.'

John Cowper Powys (1872-1963): Owen Glendower

Gwerful Mechain
(fl. 1426-1500)

The authorship of the following poem has been attributed to this poet, although there remains some doubt about this.

Gwerful was the daughter of Hywel Vaughan of Fychan and it seems that she was a highly sensual woman. One of her poems, for example, describes the male sex organ.

This poem has been translated and edited by Margaret G. Lloyd from a manuscript deposited at the National Library of Wales. As is usual in editing early Welsh poetry the orthology has been modernised.

Asking for a Harp

I am Gwerful of Fferi,
from the edge of the water.
I keep the Fferi custom,
faultless tavern, rich, fine place.
The men who come with silver
I welcome in a bright robe
faithfully, for I desire
a perfect world for my guests,
singing of intimate songs
in their midst, while pouring mead.
Filling the room, there's no joy,
this host has need of a harp.
When I thought where, gracious gift,
I could get a horsehair harp,
I dispatched a messenger
to Ifan ab Dafydd's house,
baron freely giving bread,
barons his noble forebears.
I will get it from close blood,
kinsman to the best in Rhos.
Ifan would not refuse kin;
his kinswoman seeks this gift.
A loom would make me happy,
if it had a horsetail warp,
a full row of wooden pegs
from one end to the other,
tuning key in its corner
which goes wherever it goes,
a neck like that of a goose,
and a full and narrow back.
This poem secures the gift
and Ifan will bestow it.
I'll give Ifan roast and mead
if he will come to this place,
welcome when the cuckoo sings,
his dinner for two pennies.

'The Bountiful'

Gwerful Hael, or 'The Bountiful', was born in the early part of the 15th century at Blodwel, in the parish of Llanyblodwel, Shropshire. She was the daughter of Madog ab Maredydd ab Llewelyn Ddu, of the line of Tudor Trevor. Her charities were so great as to obtain for her the title of 'bountiful'. She was married first to Rhys ab Dafydd ab Hywel of Rhug, by whom she had two sons – Hywel and Gruffydd; secondly, to Gruffydd ab Ieuan Vychan of Abertanat, by whom she had one only son David, heir to the Tanat estates, who was a great patron and favourite of the bards and minstrels of his time. The families of Abertanat and Brogyntyn trace their descent from Gwerfyl Hael as also do the Salisbury's of Rhug and Llewenni; Pugh, of Mathafarn; Pryse, Gogerddan; Sir W.W. Wynn; and the Godolphin family by intermarriage with the Tanat's. She was buried in the chancel at Llanfihangel in Blodwel, now called Llanyblodwel. Guto'r Glyn, an eminent contemporary poet, wrote an elegy upon her death, setting forth her many excellencies and charities, ending with the lines –

Y bedd lle mae'i hannedd hi
A lanwed o haelioni;
O thelir pwyth i haelion,
Taler ei haelder i hon.

(Charity fills the grave she now dwells in; if the bountiful are recompensed, may this one receive the recompense of her bountifulness.) Lewis Glyn Cothi, another poet of that period, also wrote her elegy describing the general lamentation that existed in consequence of her death, and that such was the excellency of her character that she was deserving of being canonized, and of pilgrimages being made to her shrine.

Richard Williams: Montgomeryshire Worthies (1894)

The Primrose

Being at Montgomery Castle, upon the hill, on which it is situate

Montgomery Castle, was the home of Magdalen, Lady Herbert, mother of the poets George Herbert and Edward, Lord Herbert of Cherbury.

Upon this Primrose hill,
Where, if Heav'n would distill
A shoure of raine, each severall drop might goe
To his owne primrose, and grow Manna so;
And where their forme, and their infinitie
Make a terrestriall Galaxie,
As the small starres doe in the skie:
I walke to finde a true Love; and I see
That 'tis not a mere woman, that is shee,
But must, or more, or lesse than woman bee.

Yet know I not, which flower
I wish; a sixe, or foure;
For should my true-Love lesse than woman bee,
She were scarce any thing; and then, should she
Be more than woman, shee would get above
All thought of sexe, and thinke to move
My heart to study her, and not to love;
Both these were monsters; Since there must reside
Falshood in woman, I could more abide,
She were by art, than Nature falsify'd.

Live Primrose then, and thrive
With thy number five;
And women, whom this flower doth represent,
With this mysterious number be content;
Ten is the farthest number; if halfe ten
Belonge unto each woman, then
Each woman may take halfe us men;
Or if this will not serve their turne, Since all
Numbers are odde, or even, and they fall
First into this, five, women may take us all.

John Donne (1572-1631)

Portrait of a Country Gentleman

The Blayney family of Gregynog were one of the most distinguished families in Powys. Arthur Blayney, whose life is described here, was the last in line in the family tree and died unmarried in 1795. He is buried at Tregynon.

Arthur Blayney, of Gregynog, Esquire, was descended from Brochwel Ysgythrog, a Prince of Powys, in the seventh century, but he valued himself on his pedigree no otherwise than by taking care that his conduct should not disgrace it. In the early part of his life he had applied to the study of the law, not with any professional view, but merely to guard himself and those who consulted him from chicanery and injustice, to which many who made the profession their livelihood were in his opinion so strongly tempted and inclined that he seldom mentioned a lawyer without expressive marks of dislike; but this could be humour only. He read much, and had a good collection of books, but was more disposed to conceal than to obtrude his knowledge. He was a firm adherent to the Constitution under which he lived, and never spared his zeal and support when the public stood in need of it. At the same time his loyalty did not preclude him from using that invaluable privilege of a British subject in severely censuring, upon proper occasions, both the measures and instruments of Government. Uncorruptible himself, he detested venality in others. He was of no party but that of honest men. Whether he supposed that the Peerage was degenerated, and that some degree of contagion dwelt near a Court, or whether he had gathered the prejudice from history, in which he was conversant; but certain it is, he was by no means partial to Lords of Placement. No man thought more highly of Parliaments, but pertinaciously he declined the honour of representing his native county, though often invited to do so by the unbiased suffrages of his countrymen. To his small tenants he was a bountiful master, and he complained of the bad state of a cottage he shewed me, which in any other place might have been thought a good one. He applied a little land to each to keep their cow in the summer, and in the winter he gave them hay to support it. Nor was it his own property that he was desirous of improving only. The country at large he looked upon as having a peculiar claim upon him, and no undertaking was proposed but met with his countenance and liberality. The roads in particular for many miles round owe their creation almost entirely to him, and when his land was wanted to widen them, he would give it on one condition only, 'That they took enough'. You had only to convince him of the utility of a design to be sure of his purse and protection. He always took time to consider and enquire, but from the moment he was decided he wanted no subsequent instigation. His charity was liberal and diffusive; but instead of confining it to the idle vagrant and clamorous poor, his chief aim was to put deserving objects in the way, to afford them the means of providing for themselves. There are many respectable tradesmen and gentlemen, too, whose embarrassments have been removed by his friendly assistance. He was undoubtedly an economist on system, which enabled him to do what he did. When the object of expense was a proper one he never regarded the sum; of course, nothing sordid or niggardly could be imputed to him, even when economy was most conspicuous. He would never be persuaded to keep a carriage, and very seldom hired one, performing, till his infirmities disabled him, his longest journeys on horseback. His constant residence was at Gregynog, except occasional excursions to his other house at Morvill, near Bridgnorth. One of the most prominent features in his character was his hospitality, of which there are few such instances now remaining. His table was every day plentifully covered with the best things the country and season afforded, for, unless it was to do honour to particular guests, he never indulged in far-sought delicacies, preferring the ducks and chickens of his poor neighbours, which he bought in all numbers, whether he wanted them or not, and I remember in the summer of 1793 a small pond near the house swarming with the former kind; but he was very choice in his liquors, which were the best that care and money could procure. His place, not happy in situation, was neither elegant nor ornamented, but comfortable in the most extended sense of the word; inasmuch that it would be difficult to find another house where the visitor was more perfectly at his ease, from the titled tourist to the poor, benighted, way-worn exciseman who knew not where else to turn in either for refreshment or lodging.

Philip Yorke (1743-1804): 'Royal Tribes of Wales'

Shrouded in Mystery

The landscape painter Richard Wilson was born at Penegoes, near Machynlleth in 1713, but subsequently spent much of his youth at Mold in Flintshire.

A great deal of Wilson's life is shrouded in mystery, and there are periods in it about which we know very little. It was during these years of success, for instance, that his Welsh subjects were painted; but there is nothing in the story of his life as it is known to show whether this fact means that he spent much time in Wales at this time drawing and painting, as he had done in the neighbourhood of Rome, or whether he was partly drawing on an old stock of studies or memories as he did with all his subjects. We have to think of him with a large repertoire of subjects, sketch-books crammed with details, a mind full of knowledge of nature as well as of the craft of painting and the manner of the masters, so that he had a fund of experience on which to draw and was able to turn his hand to any subject which his own inclination or popular taste seemed to demand. Cader Idris, Snowdon, Caernarvon Castle, Castell-Dinas-Brân, near Llangollen, Wynnstay – all were subjects in Wales which he painted at the time, making several versions of each. And these were perhaps the greatest pictures of his career. He learned his craft as a landscape-painter before he left for Italy, and the style which earned him his success he formed from the study of the Italian landscape and the work of Italian painters.

Wilson's art found its highest expression in these pictures of his native Wales. For one thing they were painted when he was at the height of his powers and had the stimulus of a demand for his pictures. For another thing the Welsh landscape, with its mountains and wooded hills and ruins, offered all that a painter whose imagination had been fired by the Italian landscape could seek, and was thus easy to interpret in the language of pictures which Wilson had learned from Claude and Poussin.

David Bell (1916-1959): The Artist in Wales

Contemptible and Insignificant

In his tour account of a visit to Wales in 1795, Joseph Hucks writes of a visit to Llangynog.

Whilst we were at dinner in a little ale-house (which by the bye was the only one in the place), we had a glance at the clergyman, who happened to enter the house at that very time; his appearance altogether bespoke an inferiority of condition, disgraceful to that respectable body of which he was a member; upon observing us, he abruptly went out, while our landlady informed us, with an air of triumph, as if he was something superior to the rest of mankind, that 'that was the parson'. He was standing near the house when we went out, and wishing to enter into conversation with him, I desired him to inform me which was the direct road to Bala; he appeared somewhat confused, and waving his hand towards the way we had enquired for, answered only by the monosyllable 'that', and walked hastily away. I felt much hurt, and at the same time a great degree of admiration, both at his truly laconic answer, as well as at his manner of address, in which pride seemed to be struggling with poverty; in such a situation any degree of sensibility would be to him rather a misfortune than a blessing. Fixed to a spot in which there could be no one proper for his company, or capable of his conversation, he might be driven to pass his evenings, for the sake of society, with people very far inferior to him, and by degrees lose those finer qualities of the mind, that refinement of action as well as of thought, which properly distinguish the gentleman from the honest but blunt peasant, or the industrious mechanic. I should not have mentioned this circumstance, but that it bears some credible testimony to the common report of the shameful and scanty provision made for the Welsh clergy; which by no means enables them to assume that character so essentially necessary to the ministers of christianity. I do not wish to insinuate that there is any disgrace in poverty, but certainly the ignorant and uninstructed too frequently treat their teachers with a respect proportioned to their appearance; and if this be true, it calls loudly for laws and regulations which shall be more favourable to the lower clergy in general. The act of parliament confines the salaries of curates within twelve and fifty pounds per annum, whereas it ought to have been proportioned either to the duty performed, or the value of the benefice itself. Let us take one instance – a curate serves two churches ten miles distant from each other; whilst the incumbent, or vicar, who holds them both, and receives for the joint value of the tithes, five hundred pounds per annum, allows his curate, who does all the duty, only forty pounds per annum. This cannot be considered as an adequate compensation, even for the labour; and adding the respectability and appearance of the profession, it is indeed contemptible and insignificant.

Joseph Hucks (1772-1800): A Pedestrian Tour Through North Wales

The Permanency of the Language

In the light of the discussions on the Welsh language which have taken place within the last century and more it is interesting to read Walter Davies' comments.

The Welsh language being still spoken on the confines of Offa's Dike, is a proof of its permanency, however anxious some of the mixed or bastard tribe may be for its total extinction. The arguments brought by those who plead that one general language only should be spoken by all his majesty's subjects, may be specious enough. It would be convenient to a *few travellers*, if his majesty's good subjects in Wales were all English: but however, it can hardly be desired that a whole nation should forget their own tongue and learn another from them; the only reasonable method for removing this inconvenience would be for such persons, before they go into that country, to take care to learn Welsh.

Some advocates for the abolition of the Welsh tongue, are vain enough to prognosticate a near approaching day, when it will be numbered among the dead. They see some few families upon the borders, and about a dozen innkeepers upon the post roads, who speak English only: but there are thousands, and tens of thousands in the wilds of Wales, who have learned the language of their parents, and of their country, as naturally and as innocently as they sucked their mother's breasts, or breathed the common air: they have neither opportunity nor inclination to learn any other tongue. This is the impregnable fortress of the Welsh language, where a riveted, cordial antipathy against the English tongue, caused by the cruelties of Edward I and of the Lancastrian family, dwells as commander in chief. Storm this garrison, and overturn Snowdon from its base.

Walter Davies (Gwallter Mechain 1781-1849):
The English Works of Rev. Walter Davies, edited by Silvan Evans

The Genius of the Mountains

Derwenog dead! My generation knows little of this genius who spent his life on the mountains and who, during the last days in the frail light-headedness of his old age, could not forget the lambs and the other animals that were his companions on the hills of Maldwyn. There, on the lonely slopes of Nant-yr-eira, or on the broad hearth of Cwmderwen, he composed his *awdlau, englynion* and songs. Sometimes, in the valleys of Glamorgan, or in the vales of the north, I meet a few grey-haired men who still remember about Derwenog and his harmonium, and they remember Derwenog too, who tramped the land singing and entertaining the men and women of Wales. By now he has left us, and his tradition, I am afraid, is also fast disappearing. Shame on us if we ever lose the warm friendliness and the broad tradition which was behind it all.

I don't know how old I was when I first saw him, but I must have been very young – a six year-old lad – seeing this quiet man walking slowly towards the farm nearest my home, where his sister lived. But from that time onwards Derwenog, the old man, became a friend to me, the youngster. I always remember him as an old man – not an ancient old man, as we would say, but a man of about seventy-five, with greying hair, sure-footed but slow, his speech leisurely and his still eyes sparkling whenever he heard the click of a promising line of *cynghanedd*.

Iorwerth Peate (1901-1982): *Sylfeini*

Nant yr Eira

In memory of Derwenog and some of the members of Capel Beulah.

There are owls tonight at Dôl-y-garreg-wen,
the grass covers the yard and the walls are grey with lichen,
and the cotton-grass spreads its sheet across the garden.

The plumes are a white shroud, over Cwmderwen's bare peat-marsh,
and the two ricks are like two eyes aglow no longer,
and the stars a host of candles there on the hill's altars.

Frail white-topped dwellers on the moors, what sorry enchantment
turned each memory to a skeleton, and the ancient moor to a shrine?
None, save Time's tyranny that withers all that is fine.

The old voices will not come back to Beulah through the sore
burden of six feet of earth; too much for them to bear.
Be tranquil, bruised heart, and expect them no more.

The old gentleness you loved, it fled on unreturning ways,
it vanished with the summers, the sweetness of former days.
Nothing remains but the trembling of cotton-grass in the breeze.

Iorwerth Peate (1901-1982), translated by Joseph P. Clancy

Catherine Lloyd

Catherine Lloyd, who had fallen, by chance as it were, among the red suburban villas of Llandrindod from her native habitat on the slopes of Mynydd Epynt, was a lady who got up pretty early in the morning. And so, having found herself in such a place, she prospered. She had been in the town now for fifteen years, ever since she had lost her husband – first as a sort of companion and general help for Janet, her cousin, and then as sole mistress of Epynt. Her command over the English language, however, continued to give her trouble; and much head-shaking beneath the white frilly cap and many gestures of her long, gnarled hands were often more effective means of communication than words. Something of her native Puritanism still remained with Catherine Lloyd, but in course of time, keeping a guest-house, even a dry guest-house, had been a pretty effective means of easing the pangs of that uncomfortable syndrome. She would only act the fierce Puritan now if some poor lodger came in with a suggestion on his breath that he had frequented a species of bar less pure than a milk bar, or when Anne the maid stayed out late while a pile of super dishes awaited her. On this occasion, all the stern virtues of the past descended heavily upon the place.

Nevertheless, she would muse to herself, it was quite remarkable how modern her ideas were, considering how old-fashioned her upbringing had been. Not that, hopefully, she was one whit the less religious. But it was such a different age, especially in a modern place like Llandrindod, with landladies in cut-throat competition with each other. And then there were the prodigal light-headed maids, so expensive to keep. No Christian woman could live honestly in such a place – and pay her way. For her part, whoever wished to could go to chapel; her religion, for years now, had been to slave away, day in, day out, so that others might have the benefit. Who could begin to appreciate a landlady's world?

D.J. Williams (1885-1970): The Mecca of the Nation, translated by R. Gerallt Jones and included in 'The Penguin Book of Welsh Short Stories', edited by Alun Richards

A Love Story

Margiad Evans was an English writer who lived in Bridstow, near Ross-on-Wye for sixteen years. Living in border country had a profound influence on her and this is very apparent in her writing. Her view of the Welsh marches as a region where torn allegiances are still very much alive finds its most explicit expression in her novel Country Dance, *which is set in the nineteenth century.*

Sian Pritchard from Glanrafon (on the banks of the river) is married to Abel Daw in the chapel at Pentredwr to-day. He keeps a draper's shop in Salus. Her father is fair furious at the marriage, being a true Welshman that would have his daughter marry one of her own country, but her English mother is well content the girl should go back over the Border.

Five years ago this July, Abel comes to Glanrafon in the evening with a pack on his shoulders as a journeyman. Mrs Pritchard was that overjoyed to make welcome one of her own country that she kept him the night over, and by candle-light he and Sian cast such looks at each other as they neither of them ever forgot. The next year Abel came again to ask Sian if she would be his wife, and she said she would. He had started his shop, but when her father came to hear of it he fell into a rage, and went at Abel with a flail before Sian, till he was all but dead had she not dropped down in a fit on the threshing floor. She was so mortal ill that her father swore he would never thwart her or cross her again, so be she got better. For years Abel never came near her; at last she sent him a letter, and now for his promise Mr Pritchard must put up with the wedding.

These last evenings I have been making her lace for a present. Mary went to the chapel; she said the lace was sewn on the wedding dress.

When the sun is down and the day cools off towards nightfall, Gabriel and I go up to Graig Ddu. He has his dog and his crook with him, and in his hand is a bottle of Thorley's, which makes me think of the master.

'Ben is in for the trials at Pentredwr. You'll be coming, Ann? It's not like a celebration,' says he.

'Yes. I'll be there.'

'You shall see us win the cup from the Caernarvonshire bitch.'

We stop at the pool where we was used to catch trout.

'Could you catch them in your hands now?' he asks.

It is already dusk when we are among the sheep. Ben fetches them together in the hollow called the Basin, and Gabriel and I sit down on a rock and wait for the moon to rise.

'Gwen Powys gives me but a scrap of candle for the lantern, so when there is free light I use it. She is the nearest woman in these parts, and many of them are near enough, God knows! She stints for food and light and firing. She keeps a sharp eye on the almanac too, and at full moon my candle is shorter by an inch, be the weather fair or foul. The mountain is well named Graig Ddu (Black Mountain). I have been up and down these paths on some dark nights, Ann.'

'Have you seen the Roman soldiers marching through Craig Dinas and the White Lady that drowned herself in Llyn-tro?' (the turning pool).

'Never, and I have fished it many a night alone. All I heard was an otter splashing off the bank. It's a lonely place after dark under those trees, with the water rushing over the stones. There's never hardly much of a moon down there.'

I cannot see his face, but his voice changes after a moment. He points down where we came from.

'There are no lights in Tan y Bryn, you see? Gwen Powys sits by the hearth knitting stockings in the dark to save candles, and if Megan and Margiad are not out visiting or courting, they have to go to bed. It's well for them they are handsome girls.'

'You speak discontented, Gabriel,' I says, thinking he has good reason for it.

'I have worked here fifteen years, and now I have done with Wales – done with it. Come spring we will be married. Perhaps I can find a place over the Border, where candle-ends count for less. Ah! if I can win the trials.'

He sits there silent with his arm round my waist.

'Look,' I say, 'the moon is up, we can count the sheep.'

'There's all the night before us. Now I can see you, Ann. How beautiful you are!'

Margiad Evans (1909-1958): Country Dance

In the Hayfield

'Dew in the Grass', Eiluned Lewis' enchanting autobiographical novel of a childhood spent in Montgomeryshire, evokes vividly not only a vanished world but the essence of childhood itself. The story takes place in the Severn district between Newtown (Y Drenewydd) and Llanidloes.

. . . everyone was in the hayfield – raking the hay into windrows and gathering the windrows into cocks. The men walked in line: the children's father, Beedles, Jarman, Davey John and Twm the Weeg. Twm was Mr Gwyn's gamekeeper. He was a splendid man who carried ferrets about in bags, could tell you stories of polecats and discover the secret springs of water with nothing more than a peeled stick. The Weeg, where he lived, was away beyond the Long Moel where Lucy had never been, though Delia had sometimes ridden there on the pony with her father. Twm's face was round and red, like the sun on a frosty evening. Looking one day at Jarman's yellow skin and black hair, Lucy had asked him why his face was so different from Twm's.

'Twm's hot from walking, seemingly. The Weeg's a tidy way off,' Jarman answered rather crossly, and Lucy wished that she could have been at the Weeg early in the morning to see Twm's face before he set out to walk over the Long Moel.

To-day it was redder than ever, for the sun poured down all day on the hayfield, and the men worked with their shirts open on their chests. In the shade of the oak trees by the hedge stood the great cans of cider and the blue-and-white hooped mugs. There was tea in the hayfield for everyone: the maids carried it down from the house in big baskets and spread the white cloths on the cropped grass.

Towards evening, when the children's mother had left the field, Louisa sat in the middle of the biggest cock with Miriam asleep in her lap while Maurice ran about burying himself and calling to the others to find him. Delia worked steadily, walking behind the men and raking tidily round the cocks. So too did Lucy – for a time. But soon she grew tired; the rough handle of the rake blistered her hand; she moved too quickly so that sometimes she missed the hay altogether, and then the teeth of her rake would become embedded in the ground or entangled in the buttercup runners. At last she flung the rake away.

Eiluned Lewis (1900-1979): Dew in the Grass

My Village

James Hanley is one of the most underrated English novelists of the twentieth century. He lived in the village of Llanfechain, eight miles from Oswestry and in the county of Montgomery from 1940 until 1964.

My village wears age like an old cloak, and under it the past is as warm as a new-laid egg. But tomorrow it will be different. Tomorrow it will be raised up, bannered, will explode with light, for at last, at long last, the bright men from the town have found it. It is on their map, bright red. I can hear them talking about my village: 'That village is dying, we must come to the village.'

Their talk and their words are as bright as buttons.

'Its eye is an old stopped clock, the street is crooked, people go about in quaint, unfashionable clothes, and a farmer or two drowns under an old sack too heavy for his shoulders. And look at the children, their eyes full of blackberries.'

'Heaven alone knows with what their ears are stuffed.'

'Hay, without a doubt.'

'We will carry the light to the dead eye.'

'And when it begins to shine the crooked street will straighten itself.'

'Even the church clock will begin to strike properly, though I shan't prophesy its effect upon old ears.'

'Nor anyone else.'

These voices travel down on the wind, and the village that is bent with age can hear them. They must come then. Let them come. And they *have* come, this very day, and under its empty stare these men seem even brighter. Came in a fast red car, a sizzling, mechanical insect, and threw themselves out of it, urgent, talking fast, looking tremendously important. They are standing in the square, between the chapel and the post-office, and they are talking at speed. Tongues like razors and eyes like flints, and butterly hands that are full of cunning, without a doubt. I hear their talk, their rehearsal for the acts.

'Light for your cottage, Mrs Vaughan?'

But will she hear it with her ears full of hair?

'What is that?'

'*Light* For *your* cottage.'

Curved and shining words out of a new language, but they

break like stones at an old woman's feet.

They come nearer. She bends.

'What light?'

'Electric.'

'What is that?'

'*Light.*'

'I do not want it then.'

An aged hand is too slow for the door, and now it will not shut. A bright man's eye is on her, but his foot is like a space.

'You *see*. Take that room above. Dark. We will fill it with light.'

'Daylight is cheaper. I always said it.'

The foot withdrawn, the back turns, in disgust, in hopelessness. What can a bright man do in this village? Do they not know what progress means? They lean to the bridge, watch the water swirl by; they confer.

James Hanley (1901-1985), from an article in the journal 'Wales'

Market Day in Henberth

Islwyn Ffowc Elis is one of the most popular contemporary Welsh language writers. His Cysgod y Cryman *('The Shadow of the Sickle') is a seminal work in the field of fiction. The novel focuses on the farm of Lleifior in Montgomeryshire and many threads run through the book which reveal the author's concern with some key issues, including Communism.*

It was market-day in Henberth and the old town was wide awake. It sprang to life every Wednesday, with cars parked on both sides of the high street, the pavements almost groaning under the weight of people. English was the language spoken in Henberth all week, but on Wednesdays the countryside came into town, drowning it out with the distinctive Welsh of Powys. Every shopkeeper who could speak a little of the old language dusted it down every Wednesday, and every Thursday put it away again. Groups of farmers and their wives stood here and there, discussing the land, the weather and the price of eggs. It's warm or it's cold, we need rain or a dry spell, the heifers are dear or cheap, and someone's died or married or made a terrible mess of things. The same conversation from one group to the next, with only the names changed.

Weaving their way through the crowd there were long-legged farmers, big-bellied cattle-dealers, seed-corn salesmen who knew everyone, and the occasional auctioneer's clerk, red of face and pencil behind his ear. Shrill-voiced farmers from up-country pulling one another's legs in a torrent of Welsh, and sullen men from the lowlands talking drab sense in atrocious English. On the pavement, in the Corner Café, in the Green Lion, in the mart, and in the ironmonger's shop, Henberth had sprung to life for the day.

Edward Vaughan steered his car into a narrow gap between two others with their bonnets facing the pavement. Hardly had he got out and locked the door when he heard a voice behind him.

'Good-morning, Edward Vaughan.'

He recognized the voice and, without turning round, said, 'Good-morning, Robert Pugh.'

'You're late today.'

'Had to set the men to work before starting out. They can finish getting the hay in tomorrow if they have it ready today. You're quite close to finishing, I suppose.'

'Only the home field left. It'll be done before Sunday's out.'

'Good.'

The two stood together on the pavement. Robert Pugh took his watch out of his waistcoat pocket.

'It's nearly midday. They're about to open. No point in inviting you for a drink, is there, Edward Vaughan?'

'Still temperance, Robert Pugh. And temperance I'll be, I expect, till the end of my days.'

The folds of Robert Pugh's belly began to wobble and he chuckled.

Islwyn Ffowc Elis: Cysgod y Cryman (Shadow of the Sickle),
translated by Meic Stephens

An Unanswered Question

Manafon was an eye-opener to me. Here I became aware of the clash between dream and reality. I was a proper little bourgeois, brought up delicately, with the mark of the church and the library on me. I had seen this part of the country from the train in the evening through a romantic haze. I now found myself amongst hard, materialistic, industrious people, who measured each other in acres and pounds; Welshmen who turned their backs on their inheritance, buying and selling in Welshpool, Oswestry and Shrewsbury; farmers of the cold, bare hillsides, who dreamed of saving enough money to move to a more fertile farm on the plains. But it was in some ways an old-fashioned district. When I went there in 1942, there was not a single tractor in the area. The men worked with their hands, hoeing, sheep-shearing, collecting hay, and cutting hedges. The horse was still in use. There was a smithy there; I can hear the sound of the anvil still, and see the sparks flying. I can remember the lonely figures in the fields, hoeing or docking mangles, hour after hour. What was going on in their heads, I wonder? The question remains unanswered to this day.

R.S. Thomas (1913-2000): Selected Prose, edited by Sandra Anstey

The Next Village to Manafon

It was half past seven on Saturday night
When we stopped off at the Powys Arms.
Already the locals were half-way tight,
Red-faced men from the steep green farms.

Some talked of girls and country pleasures
And some were grumbling about the hay
And some were discussing the bardic measures,
Heirs of Owain Cyfeiliog they.

We kept our end up, passing strangers,
As best we could, with what tales we knew,
Avoiding the subtle verbal dangers
Laid like poachers by the deft-tongued crew.

Song for song we joined in the singing
And not for a moment the clonk did flag,
The glasses clinked and the room was ringing.
I hope God drinks, said the village wag.

It was half-past nine on Saturday night
As we broke the spell and drove over the hill.
They pressed us to stay, but we took our flight
And none too soon, or we'd be there still.

Harri Webb (1920-1994)

Saunders Lewis at Newtown

Ironically enough
it was an English chapel. Bluff
as a sandwich-board
the wall proclaimed 'Worship the Lord',
but the beauty was heard
not seen, the holiness was word –
fresh as an evening thrush
in that mahogany and plush.

Spare, nimble, Hawtrey-like,
he climbed behind the pulpit's dyke
above the sea of us
rippling below. Calm, without fuss
he took his stance, began
his panegyric, preaching Ann,
Ann and her wheeling words
brushing Wales like a spring of birds.

Farmer, professor, knight,
Dominican and Carmelite,
you, the predestinate,
I, the stranger within the gate,
all made one by the word,
the voice, the song, the singer, heard
Ann's sacred nightingales
chant in the cupola of Wales.

Raymond Garlick

On the Border, Llanymynech
(for John Osmond)

Cwms ice-gouged, crags churned smooth,
ramparted, castellated, spilled and busted:
this ripped old seam of hard highland / fruity plain
is contention's cradle, from the grind pre-human
of glacial strife to a squall between neighbours
    – Taffy was a Welshman –
over something somehow seriously more
than a dodged round, the match or a girl.

    Voices at the Lion,
where I can drink in Wales and piss in England,
are a brandied agricultural gruel, wayward their slither
with Cymru's names; yet antennae long picksome
nail this transient straight as Deheubarth born
    – Taffy was a Welshman –
(and a *hwntw*, he must own, too dumb in *Cymraeg*
to treat even, in depth, of the weather).

Ac Offa geslog . . . swa hit Offa geslog . . .
They came yes they carved up Ynys Prydain,
they sliced us top and toe from cymric kin:
    strangers, welisc:
Offa struck with his sword the boundary out.
    And the elegies, aren't they
doing us to death? Say instead that Offa's line
marks Offa's retreat, that here at least
is where the rot stops . . . Say it, and hear it
    rattles back at you
    in the tongue of guess who
from out of our country's hollowed heart . . .

    A cheery Sais, for the camera,
straddles the line: a foot, for once, in both camps
and his balls, he laughs, in no-man's land . . .
I, called to pose, sit where I sit: for the march and its
crazings – a metre, a mile, a continent away –
    I carry within.

'Too long,' he says, 'your border so-called . . .
Not a bad try, though, fair play. But Berlin, Maastricht,
the fences are falling. It's quitsville, eh? Cornwall time,
    shopping and golf . . .
    A pint of Draig Wen?'

    Mine's a Guinness, the tart savour
of a people who dared, and a whisky to chase it
for the thistle winding free.
To memory I drink, and the burn of desire,
to bounds re-found and an end to the centuries'
    spill and blur:
that we may rise, as of old, re-made re-making,
and visioned anew for use in the world.
'You're talking,' he says, 'like some Chechen . . . '
    and so, *nos da*, perhaps I am.
I drain my glass, take a last piss in England,
    and upward gyre
to sleep among the rafters I know not where.

Nigel Jenkins

73

Emu's Egg

Trudging through rain along the windy hill
to pull a snarled-up lamb, whistle the dogs
to their flat-our looping of the ewes,
he nursed the notion of Australia –
heat, space, a chance of more
than his hard-earnied Breconshire pittance.
Idea became plan, was told,
marvelled at, acted on. He was best friend
to my old neighbour's grandfather,
turned to him for help – a horse and cart
to Liverpool. Northwards they rattled,
through Builth, Newtown, Welshpool. At Liverpool
came a fraught moment. 'John', he said,
tears not far, 'John, sell the horse and cart,
come with me!' For a moment
that far-off sun shone for his friend too,
coaxing; then it was dimmed
by green damp, more deeply penetrating.
'No', said John, 'I can't, I can't'; turned south
through Welshpool, Newtown, Builth again.

John was dead by the time
a letter came, and an Australian parcel,
exotic, unique – an emu's egg,
black, the size (his children said)
of two teacups put together.
It stayed at the farm for years,
then got broken. For a while
they saved the fragments of shell; the story
lasted a little longer. Unlikely transmitter,
I set it down, feeling perhaps for both
brave dreamer and chicken-hearted friend –
one who forced a dream to live, and one
who missed for ever his black two-teacup egg.

Ruth Bidgood

A Malignant Power

Here we find Robert Roberts at Castle Caereinion once more, this time observing clerical life.

I had no need to go far to find that the Rector's name stank in the nostrils of all the people. I never knew a man so thoroughly hated by all classes alike. They were nearly all churchpeople, especially the natives: the few dissenters that were there were new arrivals from the hills; but though almost everybody went to church, at least occasionally, the active hatred shown towards the clergyman far surpassed anything I had ever known or heard of in those parts of Wales where the mass of people are Dissenters. There the parson was passively disliked, or rather his ministrations only were disliked, while, personally, there was no disfavour shown towards him; here it was the person that was hated. He was a malignant power, ever present among them, and as they averred, ever doing harm. Hats were taken off before his face, but 'curses not loud but deep' were always heard wherever his name was mentioned. I was ambitious enough, and would have liked eight hundred a year as well as most people, but would not have taken double the money to be hated as intensely as the Rector of Castle was by his parishioners.

The curate was very harmless and inoffensive, and quite cowed by the rector's superior energy. He was not much liked or respected, for he was too featureless a man to inspire much liking for; but you could endure his presence without feeling a tingling in your right toe, so that if we did not much care for him, we did not detest him. He had to open the school daily with prayer, and when late, which happened sometimes, had to bear a public scolding from the rector, who generally happened to look in on those late mornings. He bore it all very meekly, poor fellow, but I am sorry to say that I gave him no credit for that Christian virtue of meekness, but rather despised him therefor. I soon found out that he was horribly tyrannized over by the Rector. Every day he had to make his appearance at the Rectory to receive orders with respect to visits, and general parochial work, and woe betide him if any of the work cut out for him was neglected. The Sunday's sermon had always to be gone over on the previous Saturday in the presence of the Rector – and it was said of the Rectoress, too – but I cannot vouch for the truth of this. I had often entertained some ambitious thoughts of becoming a clergyman myself, but when I thought of the servitude of the poor curate of Castle, I doubted whether I might not be better off as I was, if such a rigorous apprenticeship as that was necessary before one could reach the milk and honey of a living.

Robert Roberts (1834-1885):
The Life and Opinions of a Wandering Scholar

Brambleton Hall

The Expedition of Humphrey Clinker *relates, through a series of letters, the adventures of a family as they travel through England and Scotland.*
The following extract comes from a letter addressed to her housekeeper by Tabitha Bramble of Brambleton Hall on the Welsh side of the border near Crickhowel.

. . . as we are drawing homewards, it may be proper to uprise you that Brambleton Hall may be in a condition to receive us after the long journey. By the first of next month you may begin to make constant fires in my brother's chamber and mine; and burn a faggot every day in the yellow damask room: have the tester and curtains dusted, and featherbed and matresses well aired, because, perhaps, with the blessing of heaven, they may be used on some occasion. Let the old hogsheads be well skewered and seasoned . . .

If the house was mine, I would turn over a new leaf. I dont see why the servants of Wales should not drink fair water, and eat hot cakes and barley cale, as they do in Scotland, without troubling the butcher above once a quarter . . . As you must have laid a great many more eggs than could be eaten, I do suppose there is a great many more eggs than would be eaten, I do suppose there is a power of turkeys, chickens, and guzzling about the house; and a brave kergo of cheese ready for market . . .

Pray let the whole house and furniture have a thorough cleaning from top to bottom; for the honour of Wales . . .

Tobias Smollet (1721-1771): The Expedition of Humphrey Clinker

Shelley at Cwm Elan

During the summer of 1811 Percy Bysshe Shelley spent several weeks at Cwm Elan, south west of Rhayader, with cousins. The following year found Shelley back at the home of his cousins, the Grove family, this time with his wife Harriet. They decided to make a home here and acquired Nantgwyllt, a large house in two hundred acres of grounds. But their stay was brief and came to an abrupt end when Shelley realised that the lease was too expensive.

The Elan reservoir drowned the valley some years ago.

What follows is a letter which the poet wrote from Cwm Elan during the 1811 visit. It is addressed to Elizabeth Hitchener.

. . . This country of Wales is excessively grand; rocks piled on each other to tremendous heights, rivers formed into cataracts by their projections and valleys clothed with woods, present an appearance of enchantment but *why* do they enchant, *why* is it more affecting than a plain, it cannot be innate, is it acquired? – Thus does knowledge lose all the pleasure which involuntarily arises, by attempting to arrest the fleeting Phantom as it passes – vain – almost like the chemist's aether it evaporates under our observation; it flies from all but the slaves of passion and sickly sensibility who will not analyse a feeling. I will relate you an anecdote, it is a striking one; the only adventure I have met with here. My window is over the kitchen; in the morning I threw it up, and had nearly finished dressing when 'for Charity's dear sake' met my ear, these words were pronounced with such sweetness that on turning round I was surprised to find them uttered by an old beggar, to whom the servant brought some meat, I ran down and gave him something: he appeared extremely grateful. I tried to enter into conversation with him – in vain. I followed him a mile asking a thousand questions; at length I quitted him finding by this remarkable observation that perseverance was useless. 'I see by your dress that you are a rich man – they have injured me and mine a million times. You appear to be well intentioned but I have no security of it while you live in such a house as that, or wear such clothes as those. It wd. be charity to quit me.'

P.B. Shelley (1792-1822): The Letters of Percy Bysshe Shelley, edited by F.L. Jones (1964)

Parted

The novelist Hilda Vaughan was born in Builth Wells. Some of her fiction is set in Radnorshire, including A Battle of the Weak *and* The Invader. *Her novella* A Thing of Nought *is a tale of star-crossed love set in the hills of Elfael in the southern region of the county.*

It was not until the autumn, when Penry had gone away, that Megan began to realize the meaning of that dread word 'parted'. Then her longing to see him and to hear his voice became a physical torment, and she would be awake at night struggling with her sobs, telling herself in vain that this separation was but for a little time.

The winter set in pitiless. For months the pass at the top of the valley was snowbound, and even the pious few who attended Alpha chapel in lonely Cwmbach were kept from their devotions. Megan went about her household duties day by day, silent and subdued, finding the weeks and months of waiting, which were to have sped by so swiftly, intolerably long. She wrote to Penry every Saturday night; but letter-writing was to her a labour, exceedingly slow and toilsome and when the ill-spelt letters, that had cost such pains, were returned to her long after, with 'Not known at this address' scrawled on them, she abandoned herself to despair. It seemed as though she would never hear from Penry, never be able to reach him, now that the unknown had closed upon him. She tormented herself with the thought that he had died on the voyage out; until at last, almost a year after he had gone away, she received his first letter. It was despondent in tone, but still she hugged it to her as evidence that he was still alive, and not irrevocably lost to her.

He had arrived in Australia, so he wrote, to find that his uncle was dead, and that no work was to be obtained in that locality. There had been a succession of droughts, and prospects were very bad; still, he had managed, after great difficulty, to find temporary employment on a sheep ranch. He feared that making a home for his Megan would prove a longer business than they had thought, but, if she would wait from him, he would never give up the struggle.

Wait for him? What else could he fancy there was for her to do? What was she living for but the time when they should meet again? She laughed at him for imagining that she could ever give any other man a thought. She carried his letter about inside her bodice, and slept with it under her pillow, until it was tattered and crumpled. Then, lest she should wear it out altogether, she put it away in the oak chest where she kept the coloured daguerreotype he had sent her of himself before he sailed from Liverpool. It was her most cherished possession, too well beloved to be exposed; to be taken out and looked at only by lamplight and in secret.

Another year went by, and another; and after that, in her loneliness and disappointment, Megan lost count of the seasons that divided her from her lover, and, at length, even from hope. She heard from him at rare intervals. Now he was doing well, and would soon have earned enough to come and fetch her. Now another drought had ruined his employer, and he was again cast on the world, searching for work, whilst his precious store of savings, that meant happiness for them both, dwindled.

He had been gone seven years when she received a short, barely legible letter, written in pencil, much blurred, and in a laboured, childish hand. Luck was against him. She must wait for him no longer. He had been almost starving for the last month, rather than break into the store of money he had laid by. He had enough to come and fetch her now, but where was the good in bringing her out to a country in which he had no home to offer her? Every enterprise he touched failed. He had begun to think that he brought ill fortune with him wherever he went. 'Like Jonah in the Bible,' he wrote. 'I won't never bring you, my love, to ruin, you may be sure. So better think of me as dead.' There followed a cross and his signature.

This was the last letter she ever received from him . . .

Hilda Vaughan (1892-1985): A Thing of Nought

An Extraordinary Vicar

The Rev. John Price became vicar of Llanbedr-Painscastle in 1859.

The stipend was meagre, and there was no vicarage: Price live in three old bathing machines, which served respectively as study, bedroom and kitchen. After these were accidentally burnt down he dwelt in a brick and slate hen-house. The parishioners, mostly dissenters, did not find their way to church. Interpreting literally the parable of the Marriage Feast, he went out to the highways and hedges to procure guests for his spiritual banquet; and soon an offer of sixpence per head per service began regularly to fill his pews with unwashed tramps and their draggle-tailed doxies. Later, when he lost a tiny private income, this had to be reduced to fourpence. This new proposal was solemnly discussed in the churchyard, and finally accepted by a sort of informal Tramps' Union. For the comfort of his flock in winter he provided oil stoves; cooking was allowed during the sermon. Price further offered five shillings to each pair of vagrants 'living in sin' who would consent to let him join them in Holy Wedlock. As his sight was very weak, several business-like couples let him marry them half a dozen times. Having sunk into a very neglected state, he was taken by friends to Talgarth, where it was found necessary to cut his clothes off his skin. He did not survive the bath which followed.

Thoresby Jones: Welsh Border Country (undated)

Kilvert Visits the Solitary

In this green cwm stood a little grey hut. It was built of rough dry stone without mortar and the thatch was thin and broken. At one end of the cabin a little garden had been enclosed and fenced in from the waste. There was one other house in sight where the cwm lay open to the west, Pencommon which used to belong to Price, the old keeper, who died lately in Clyro Village. Not a soul was stirring or in sight on the hill or in the valley, and the green cwm was perfectly silent and apparently deserted. As we turned the corner of the little grey hut and came in sight of the closed door we gave up all hope of seeing the Solitary and believed that our pilgrimage had been in vain. Then what was my relief when I knocked upon the door to hear a strange deep voice from within saying, 'Ho! Ho!' There was a slight stir within and then the cabin door opened and a strange figure came out. The figure of a man rather below the middle height, about 60 years of age, his head covered with a luxuriant growth of light brown or chestnut hair and his face made remarkable by a mild thoughtful melancholy blue eye and red moustache and white beard. The hermit was dressed in a seedy faded greasy suit of black, a dress coat and a large untidy white cravat, or a cravat that had once been white, lashed round his neck with a loose knot and flying ends. Upon his feet he wore broken low shoes and in his hand he carried a tall hat. There was something in the whole appearance of the Solitary singularly dilapidated and forlorn and he had a distant absent look and a preoccupied air as if the soul were entirely unconscious of the rags in which the body was clothed.

The Solitary came forward and greeted us with the most perfect courtesy and the natural simplicity of the highest breeding. 'And now,' he said thoughtfully, 'how shall we do? My landlord promised at 2 o'clock to meet me in an hour's time on the hill with a gambo to bring home my mawn.' It was now 3 o'clock.

I asked if he would allow us to accompany him up to the mawn hill. 'Would you like it?' he said eagerly. 'Would you like it?' Then he went off with Williams to Pencommon to stable 'the mare' begging me to wait and sit down in his house till he returned. 'The house' was a sight when once seen never to be forgotten. I sat in amazement taking mental notes of the strangest interior I ever saw. Inside the hut there was a wild confusion of litter and rubbish almost choking and filling up all available space. The floor had once been of stone but was covered thick and deep with an accumulation of the dirt and peat dust of years. The furniture consisted of two wooden saddle-seated chairs polished smooth by the friction of continual sessions, and one of them without a back. A four-legged dressing table littered with broken bread and meat, crumbs, dirty knives and forks, glasses, plates, cups and saucers in squalid hugger-mugger confusion. No table cloth. No grate. The hearth foul with cold peat ashes, broken bricks and dust, under the great wide open chimney through which stole down a faint, ghastly sickly light. In heaps and piles upon the floor were old books, large Bibles, commentaries, old-fashioned religious disputation, C.M.S. Reports and odd books of all sorts, Luther on the Galatians, etc. The floor was further encumbered with beams and logs of wood, flour pans covered over, and old chests. All the other articles of food were hung up on pot hooks some from the ceiling, some in the chimney out of the way of the rats. The squalor, the dirt, the dust, the foulness and wretchedness of the place were indescribable, almost inconceivable. And in this cabin thus lives the Solitary of Llanbedr, the Revd. John Price, Master of Arts of Cambridge University and Vicar of Llanbedr Painscastle.

Francis Kilvert (1840-1879): Diary

The Radnor Hermit

I

A spectacular gorge, a waterfall; and high
up in the rocks a cavern once lived in by
an eighteenth century hermit. The walls still show
some traces of graffiti. It's worth the slow
ascent. We leave the single farm and pale
grey path and force an unmarked way now, scale
on hands and knees the laddered boles of trees
flung face down over nothing from the scree.
Above the Falls the chill of a ravine.
Surely this foetid crack could not have been
the legendary cave – In turn we stand
heads stooped inside, and try to understand:
men were smaller then, and one could lie
along this ledge, lit by a shard of sky –
The usual urinous smell. Nothing to see
other than his scribbled legacy,
a mesh of marks too faint to do as much
as raise a single ghost beneath our touch.

II

The creature's come down to the farm again –
she hears him in the yard, beside the pen,
and glimpses as the moon escapes its pall
his face hung like a cheese against the wall.
She puts out milk to placate this restless shade
of night, to keep off blight and rot – afraid
because she does not always brave the cold
descent to church on Sundays. And so she holds
through superstition his life in her hands,
coaxing through the winter its fragile strands.

The boy's cunning is only that of a brute
driven by hunger to beg; he is just astute
enough to know he needs a refuge where
they will not hunt his lunacy. And there
his solitude, unknown to him, creates
in time a being from another state –
he ages through two centuries to a seer,
his legend more deeply rooted with each year
that passes – its stature mirrored in the Falls,
their lastingness, their noise which deafens all
the wind's attempts to intimate its own
translation of the scratches in the stone.

Caroline Price

'The Dartmoor Shepherd'

In the reign of Queen Victoria, in the year 1849, one destined to stir the British public to its depths, and to make Cabinet Ministers pause in their high occupation of State affairs to listen to his cry for clemency, was born in the little cottage named Tynybwlch (meaning the house in the hollow), in the parish of Llanfihangel, in the county of Montgomery, four miles or so from the little town of Llanfyllin. That one was David Davies, son of a farm labourer of that name. The cottage is long since in ruins, and the family lived in other cottages afterwards. It was on November the Fifth – Guy Fawkes' Day – that David was born, and in after life he often referred in a jocular way to that questionable mark of distinction at his birth.

Looking back upon the career of the infant David, there is no gainsaying the fitness of things that David's arrival should have been heralded by fireworks, which in days of yore consisted for the most part of Chinese crackers. Little did David ken that he was born unto trouble as the sparks fly upward, but he was. In fifty-five years he received sentences aggregating sixty-one years three months and fifteen days, apart from weeks on remand, awaiting trial deducted from the sentences, David must have lived in prison quite fifty years. He made more than a hundred appearances before local magistrates and Assize judges.

Sir George Lambert, addressing London Devonians in 1924, drew this pen-picture of David Davies, and it was realistic of the subject in every particular. This is what Sir George said of David Davies:

'I was once at Princetown Gaol, and there I saw a benign individual radiating kindness from every pore. The sheep came at his call, and some vandals have called him the 'Dartmoor Shepherd'. At Princetown, David Davies was a pattern character, and when he went back to the Welsh hills he was a Welsh saint, with a passion for contemplating churches.'

David Davies was the most notorious gaol-bird of his age, and there was no church robber to compare with him for sacrilegious outrages.

A. Scriven: The Dartmoor Shepherd: Fifty Years in Prison
(undated)

The Pathos In It

The poet and novelist David Constantine has written a documentary novel based on the life of David Davies.

In the counties of Flint and Montgomery, Denbigh, Shropshire and Cheshire, said Bone, in hollow trees, in walls, flues, tombs and under the sod, he had hidden the proceeds of an arduous life. His convictions were many, but his offences were infinite, and in the Dock his appearances were legion but as nothing beside his non-appearances, and though his cack-handedness was legendary that of the Authorities deserved no lesser fame, and for every heavy hand on the shoulder or truncheon blow on the head, for every manacling, there were, he had boasted, a hundred going scot-free, and for every penny returned to its rightful owner or taken to pay his board, there was, he had bragged, a sovereign in a cocoa-tin or wrapped in oilskin or a bit of rag and given into the safekeeping of some hidey-hole. And though his expenses were great, on ale and railways, his savings were greater, and although during his long time a-waiting the face of the countryside changed under Acts of God, such as landslide and flood, and Works of Man, such as pits and quarries and the building of Unions, causing many a cache to be lost, its vicinity become unrecognisable, yet those remaining were more and were for ever augmented on his travels, his visits to the parishes, his furtive comings and goings, through the breaking and entering of Churches, the forcing of cupboards, the prising the lids of the Poor, in these scandalous ways, he had said, said Bone, his hoards were added to, for the child of his loins, for the peace and quiet of his old age, or for the journeying to some place of his redemption, once the trying and failing here was manifestly done. And at the end of the day, said Bone, that garnering of the sheaves, that calling the sheep to fold etc., that tallying of the sovereigns, what pathos there was in it . . .

David Constantine: Davies (1985)

The Lost Kingdom

When I was an innocent boy
my world was marvellously full,
the sun would come from Neint-hirion yard
at dawn to the gossamer meadow,
and would set over Brynaerau
where the rain and the wind sheltered –
a day's journey between the fair fortresses
of my world of wonders long ago.

If any pain or worry came,
their penance would be short.
What weariness that was not soon forgotten
amongst all the miracles of my parish?
A crusading romance in the clarion
of hunters on the manor ffridd,
daring across a sea when I carried
my pack over shallow Clegyr.

A giant came to my blameless province
and led me off on an exile's journey:
the magic that flowed once
from the vast meadow-lands is but a memory.
The grey years shattered
each fortress with their busy fingers:
nothing remains but dreams,
nothing of all the fullness.

Returning today, a weary fugitive
from iron bars;
and there I saw no creature
bending the knee to his ruler.
There was but a golden autumn
gathering the countryside's fruit,
and Time, the old enemy,
dancing on my father's grave.

Iorwerth Peate (1901-1982): translated by R. Gerallt Jones

Churning

Geraint Goodwin was born in Newtown. In his youth he became a local newspaper reporter but later went to London and worked in Fleet Street. Later in life he met Edward Garnet who became his mentor and in 1936 his well known novel, The Heyday of the Blood *appeared.*

Beti had been churning, but the butter would not 'break'. The old blue painted churn, with its bright brass fittings, had been going round and round for an hour. It was hard work too, for one so slight, but she did not mind this. The dairy stone-flagged, with an old latticed window with a wild elder before it, was the quietest place in the house.

She could think about all sorts of things there, because when she was churning there was nothing to do but think. The body went lax, but for the weight on the one arm, and the mind went floating off. The trouble was that it went leaping about like a flame in the wind, no sooner touching one thing that it was off to another. There was no weight to it at all; it went off into space.

It was only when the butter did not 'break' after an hour or so that she dropped out of this fantastic place and came down to earth like a stone. You *felt* the butter as it 'gathered', the solid weight of it on the handle of the churn, on the pressure on the palm of the hand. The exhilaration of that moment, so long awaited, was one that neither time nor custom ever destroyed. But when it did not 'break' all sorts of doubts and worries came crowding in, breaking up the peace of it all.

And now the butter did not 'break', but Gwenno would be down soon to take her turn. She was the village girl who had come in as extra help – broad as a bullock with strong rough hands and a round, red face, raw and ripe as a pippin. Gwenno had no fears at all; nothing worried her.

Beti wished she was like Gwenno; she felt that her mother wished so to. But her father never reproached her by word or look, though the Tudors were all as sturdy as oaks. But then it was no good thinking of her father; there was no beginning and no end to him.

The old churn squelched away. It had been a hard week and she was very tired. The 'jentlemens' made a lot of extra work, and yet the routine of the farm, of the house, went on just the same.

Monday was the washing day. There was a great cistern in the yard cut out of solid stone and fed by a spout from a spring. The lead spout was knocked sideways and diverted into the yard and the great cistern filled with water from the boiler. The three women would stand around patting and clouting the clothes as the Breton Peasants do. It was the same summer and winter, even though the yard cobbles were filled up with ice. And then there was all the mangling and the ironing.

Wednesday was brewing, but this was the men's affair, although the women had always to be ready to give a hand. Her father would stand, knee deep in malt, a shovel in his hand and the sweat pouring down his face. The mash was steeped from a great copper boiler, and all day long the steam rose up from the brewery door like a cloak blown upwards. It was the real *cwrw*, pure and wholesome, with a tank to it all its own. There was no coddling with, no chemical in, that brew. What the earth gave went into it – that and the clear spring water. When it was all over the mash was tipped out into the pigs-kit, and the pigs made the night sound with their snoring, lying there in a drunken stupor until far into the next day.

Geraint Goodwin (1903-1941): 'The Heyday of the Blood' (1936)

The Social Mix of Llanfihangel

Class distinction is comparatively weak in Llanfihangel and it never interferes with free social intercourse between individuals and families. Almost every family until recently has held land direct from the landlord, and therefore the division between farmer and wage-earner has been less definite than in the neighbouring lowlands with their system of tied cottages. One class merges imperceptibly into the other. One man with twenty acres may be a full-time farmer, while another with the same acreage is a roadman or forestry-worker. A childless farmer will sometimes retire to a small-holding in his old age, and will not consider it beneath his dignity to earn a little money by helping a neighbour in busy seasons. The distinction between farmers, smallholders and cottagers is one of degree rather than of kind, and it is further weakened by the custom whereby farmers' sons become farm-labourers during their youth.

Alwyn D. Rees (1911-1974): Life in a Welsh Countryside

Border Lambing

Three.
We had counted on it being quiet.
Counted less than five months
but the back-end of March can be
bitter as the horns.
A sloe-winter and a lambing snow
and the rough underbelly of the sky
snagged on the earth's thorns.

Six.
It was as if her crying had startled the wind
that tears corregate like curtain
that fills fields with every kind of voice
to shout down the clamour of the first cells.

We found her
on the sheltered side that was not shelter
with two stones for lambs
as if they had fallen from the rough lime walls.
She stood
straddling the thin sun
in the crush of earth and sky
nursing their deaths.

Whilst stables were cleared
and a makeshift shelter
made of breeze block and bales
we drove the ewes nowhere
wore a sheep-slush path to keep them
from the drifts
and from blindness.

The sheep are gathering the shepherds in
and all the world is

pied snow and sky –
kerry-faced and lapwinged.

When word came
we walked them all in willingly
save one
that stood unmoved at our
bleating and our cursing.

Ten.
The snow over.
The rookery simmering.
One star loose;
a burr on the back of the night.

I flashed a torch across their sheep-skulled
blinkered eyes and scattered their faces.

Before I slept the sky was full.
Two more had lambed
and easily enough.

Two.
She woke the half of me that slept.
I felt for the clothes I already wore,
Woke me for a lamb
buried in, backwards and swollen,
that would not pull.

In a light
peculiar to stables
she was viced by my legs
twisting to right herself
held up at the hocks.
We pulled at the hand holds;
hind hooves and tail
pulled as if we would snap that lamb away
and all the world was bleating and moaning
and the ewe was breaking like waves.
Caught in her sudden backwash

something gave something
moved, the tight noose slipped
and he broke free.

The semolina coat with a red fuse
rusted with birth-blood
the tonsured head and wishboned legs
that pegged him out for a moment
then bowed.

We left them;
her bloodied down one side
cave painting the walls
her lamb pulsing blindly for milk.

Four.
The sky's grey hollows fleeced the dawn;
necked like a jackdaw,
grazed clean of stars.
The skyline broken-mouthed
    the black jab of the lambing barns.

My world jumped and broke as if in bad animation.
'six lambed and two dead
one snowblind and scouring'.

Pale visionary faces
arms trembling from the pull
hands stiff from having gripped
too hard her wool.

One lamb in two hundred
numbered, ringed and stained
wearing the stigma in the ear.

When morning came
I could not find a shepherd's place amongst them
nor could I say if
suffering and pity mock the slaughter
or if my caring mocks me.

Andrew Morrison

The Magic of Mr Smith

The village was stuck in the valley like a stopper in a bottle. Not the Tanat valley at that point but the Rhaeadr valley; this river's sparkling waters having flown through the air from the high moors, through the waterfall, descending around a thousand corners to Llanrhaeadr, flowing under the solid wide-arched road-bridge that marked the boundary between Denbighshire and Montgomeryshire, then behind the church in a long curve, under the hanging dark trees, polishing its stony floor, until joining the Tanat, two miles away at Pedair Ffordd.

Just up from the village, set deep in woods, above the fresh waters of the Rhaeadr, was, of all things, a canal. It was man-made, a neat trough, its waters sluggish, its light brown bottom of mud clearly visible on a bright day. It ended at the turbine-house, inside which a huge metal wheel turned. When turning slowly it uttered a low groan but when the flow of water was good it turned with a happy whine. Along a path and over a stile was a field with cows. In the middle of the field was a two-storey building in pale stone. Inside its door one could see rows of dials and switches. All this was the empire of Mr Smith the Electric. When the lights went yellow and dim at home we knew that the turbine was not doing its work; too many leaves in the water, perhaps, or not enough rain. Then, oil lamps would flame into life. But at night, seldom would the wallpaper in the lounge be entirely lit so that the pattern ran all over the room. The picture-rail was stained brown and pictures hung from it from copper clasps. Flex in brown twists hung along it on tacks at Christmas and twirled around the tree in the corner. Mr Smith would call and make these arrangements. Here was a man who had moved large quantities of earth, who made a huge turbine wheel spin on its axis, who had erected wooden poles along the margins of our streets, hung heavy wires, yet there he was, with fairy-lights.

I particularly liked the round ones, but the pointed ones had their charm too. I held the round one in my hand. It was a strange colour, a creamy-white that might be the colour of well-washed sand; it was like the egg of a rare bird, but corrugated. When lit, in the corner of our room, it gave off a yellow light, inadequate according to the science of voltage, but fitting. It was part of the magic of Mr Smith.

John Idris Jones: from Berwyn Christmas
included in Christmas in Wales, edited by Dewi Roberts

A Nobody-About Place

Despite thick, mature woods and rolling downland, Radnorshire is a strangely lonely, nobody-about place, the most sparsely populated county in England and Wales. The inhabitants are not at all sure, most of them, whether they are English or Welsh and the majority, fortunately, don't seem to care. At the last count, only a handful of families said they preferred to speak Welsh. Most of the people you meet know only a few words related to place-names, such as *Gil-fach*, the little retreat, *Fron-las*, the green bank, *Pen-y-bont*, the head of the bridge, and *Sais*, which is Englishman.

What catches the ear is not so much the extraordinarily variable accent, as the inversions and idioms which come through from the Welsh. They say 'Good evening' in the afternoon. They tend to speak demonstratively 'Stay you there now and I'll ask him.' Pronouns are tossed about indiscriminately. 'So him told I you was looking for Herrock.' A Radnorshire tombstone is inscribed:

His as was has gone from we;
Us as is must go to he.

Weather is usually the first topic of conversation and fields are sometimes referred to as 'she'. 'She's not bearing well now,' they say. 'Not with that fancy dressing stuff.' Radnorshire is almost wholly agricultural. There are no industries to speak of, except for quarries. And apart from the places in the Wye Valley there are neither villages nor big country houses:

Alas, alas, Poor Radnorshire,
Never a park nor even a deer,
Never a squire of five hundred a year
Save Richard Fowler of Abby-Cwmhir.

John Hillaby: Journey Through Britain (1968)

A Radnorshire Family

Of all the people who posed outside the Red Dragon at Rhulen, that sweltering afternoon in August 1899, none had better reason for looking pleased with himself than Amos Jones, the bridgegroom. In one week, he had achieved two of his three ambitions: he had married a beautiful wife, and had signed the lease of a farm.

His father, a garrulous old cider-drinker, known round the pubs of Radnorshire as Sam the Waggon, had started life as a drover; had failed to make a living as a carter; and now lived, cooped up with his wife, in a tiny cottage on Rhulen Hill.

Hannah Jones was not an agreeable woman. As a young bride, she had loved her husband to distraction; had put up with his absences and infidelities, and, thanks to a monumental meanness, had always managed to thwart the bailiffs.

Then came the catastrophes that hardened her into a mould of unrelieved bitterness and left her mouth as sharp and twisted as a leaf of holly.

Of her five children, a daughter had died of consumption; another married a Catholic; the eldest son was killed in a Rhondda coalpit; her favourite, Eddie, stole her savings and skipped to Canada – and that left only Amos to support her old age.

Because he was her final fledgling, she coddled him more carefully than the others, and sent him to Sunday School to learn letters and fear of the Lord. He was not a stupid boy, but, by the age of fifteen, he had disappointed her hopes for his education; and she booted him from the house and sent him to earn his own keep.

Bruce Chatwin: On the Black Hill (1982)

Llanwddyn Submerged

The German writer W.G. Sebald won wide acclaim for his fictional output.

In his final novel Austerlitz *he deals with Jacques Austerlitz, a Jew who, as a young child, is sent to north Wales at the outbreak of the 1939-45 war. He is brought up by a Welsh Methodist minister and his wife in Bala and they attempt to eradicate his earlier memories, and change his name to Dafydd Elias. But his foster mother dies, while her husband becomes an inmate of the North Wales Lunatic Asylum at Denbigh.*

The image of the drowned valley is one which has a special resonance in Wales and the metaphors of this otherworld are revealed in Dafydd/Jacques' first person narrative.

. . . a kind of Old Testament mythology of retribution gradually built up inside my head, and I always saw its supreme expression in the submersion of the village of Llanwddyn beneath the waters of the Vyrnwy reservoir. As far as I can remember it was on the way back from one of his journeys to preach away from home, at either Abertridwr or Pont Llogel, that Elias stopped the pony-trap on the banks of this lake and walked out with rue to the middle of the dam, where he told me about his family home lying down there at a depth of about a hundred feet under the dark water, and not just his own family home but at least forty other houses and farms, together with the church of St John of Jerusalem, three chapels, and three pubs, all of them drowned when the dam was finished in the autumn of 1888 in the years before its submersion, so Elias had told him, said Austerlitz, Llanwddyn had been particularly famous for its games of football on the village green when the full moon shone in summer, often lasting all night and played by over ten dozen youths and men of almost every age, some of them from neighbouring villages. The story of the football games of Llanwddyn occupied my imagination for a long time, said Austerlitz, first and foremost, I am sure, because Elias never told me anything else about his own life either before or afterwards. At this one moment on the Vyrnwy dam when, intentionally or unintentionally, he allowed me a glimpse into his clerical heart, felt for him so much that he, the righteous man, seemed to me like the only survivor of the deluge which had destroyed Llanwddyn while I imagined all the others, his parents, his brothers and sisters, his relations, their neighbours, all the other villagers still down in the depths, sitting in their houses and walking along the road, but unable to speak and with their eyes opened far too wide. This notion of mine about the subaquatic existence of the people of Llanwddyn also had something to do with the album which Ebas first showed me on our return home that evening, containing several photographs of his birthplace, now sunk beneath the water. As there were no other pictures of any kind in the manse, I leafed again and again though these few photographs, which came into my own possession only much later along with the Calvinist calendar, until the people looking out of them, the blacksmith in his leather apron, Elias's father the sub-postmaster, the shepherd walking along the village street with his sheep, and most of all the girl sitting in a chair in the garden with her little dog on her lap, became as familiar to me as if I were living with them down at the bottom of the lake. At night, before I fell asleep in my cold room, I often felt as if I too had been submerged in that dark water, and like the poor souls of Vyrnwy must keep my eyes wide open to catch a faint glimmer of light far above me, and see the reflections broken by ripples, of the stone tower standing in such fearsome isolation on the wooded bank. Sometimes I even imagined that I had seen one or other of the people from the photographs in the album walking down the road in Bala, or out in the fields, particularly around noon on hot summer days, when there was no one else about and the air flickered hazily.

W.G. Sebald (1944-2001): Austerlitz
Translated by Anthea Bell

My son on Castell Dinas

Later, we walked up to the dinas holding hands.
Fosse, tump and cliff, erupted meeting place
of limestone and red sand,
grass sheepshitten and sheepcropped,
hawthorn and decaying fences.
Eastward, the track along the ridge
and all its folds of mountain falling north.
Westward, Mynydd Troed across the bwlch
hard and darkening in late afternoon.

The Cessna towed a glider overhead
snorting in laborious air.
Its shadow rippled on the pant
and the gravel droning died.

Released, he ran and played and made discoveries
and cairns and cromlechs
from the shale of fallen towers.

I saw grass and earth and stone
lichened, split, layered like the name –
castell – men in helmets holding natives down,
dinas – city before Rome breathed.
Cattle, slaves and iron bars.

A mile of air fell down towards the farms
blurring smoky in the shade.
Above the cup of land and ring of scarp,
high, the glider's lazy tilt and wheel
caught late sun on the wings,
glass teardrop of cockpit gleaming
pearly as aluminium.

He rampaged on the parapets,
slipped from my reaching hand
cartooned to thirty yards of shadow.

I watched the ridge of Mynydd Troed turn black,
the Cessna dropping in to shadow
trailing rope.

Christopher Meredith

Glyn

As far as he was aware, his mother knew nothing of the Romeo and Juliet variety of love, but she was always stressing that love, family love, was essential on a farm to make all the hard work worthwhile. 'Get yourself a nice sweetheart,' she'd beg Glyn over and over. 'And if at first you don't succeed, try, try again.'

When he was young, Glyn had put his back into the quest. But the farm was on an unclassified mountain road, eleven miles from the nearest small town, three from the nearest village and by that time girls had decent jobs in Building Societies and Estate Agents and didn't want to be farmers' wives. Or at least no-one wanted to be his wife. Even twenty years ago he was overweight and nothing of a talker. He'd persevered though, for several years, being everyone's best friend at the Young Farmers' weekly meetings, having a good laugh with all the girls, driving them here and there, buying them drinks, but never able to establish a special relationship with one of them.

'I'm giving up,' he'd announced just after Christmas one year. 'There's only so much fun a person can be doing with.'

'Don't give up,' his mother had begged. 'Please don't give up.'

He looked across at his mother's sister, his Auntie Phyllis, and her son, Hywel. Hywel was a prosperous dentist with a good practice in Newtown, a pretty wife called Jennifer and two children; a boy and a girl of course, everything falling snap into place. A good-natured chap, though, he had to admit. 'Why don't you get married, man?' he'd ask afterwards, when they were back in the lonely, isolated farmhouse. 'It's not as bad as everyone makes out and there's plenty of compensations.' 'Oh, I'm looking around,' Glyn would reply, that false, comradely note in his voice. What if he answered, 'Because no-one will bloody have me, Hywel, that's why. And why should they? I'm not handsome and self-assured like you, but flabby and tongue-tied. If I was a

98

woman, I'd run a mile sooner than have anything to do with a soft-centered bloke like me.'

Siân James: And Perhaps More included in Outside Paradise (2002)

'A Lousy Day'

Alice Thomas Ellis is one of the leading English novelists currently at work. Unexplained Laughter *is set in rural Powys and focuses on the lives of two women who are sharing a cottage and the strange goings on which occur during their stay.*

Next morning, the countryside was heavy and sullen like a house where a dreadful quarrel has taken place and still nothing is resolved. A dark palpable mist hung over the moorland and behind it the sun flamed in temper.

It was a lousy day. Everybody said so. Lydia and Betty said so, and when Lydia went into the village shop it was full of people who were saying so as well. It was the sort of day when men run their fingers round their collars and women pull their skirts away from their thighs, and people debate whether a hot cup of tea really cools you down or whether a glass of cold water is more helpful. 'It's so humid,' they moaned, and they wondered why it was that the storm had left them in this stifling, steamy condition when storms were supposed to clear the air. Even the older villagers claimed they'd never known anything like it. Some who had driven over the Berwyns insisted that they had had to put their headlights on, and this in the middle of a July day.

After a while Lydia grew bored with hearing people insulting the weather. Contrarily, she determined to find something to say in its favour. It was, after all, an unusual day, with its ominous dark mist. It made the previous days seem like shallow, callow girls, all light and bright and ordinary. 'It's not such a bad day – sort of interesting,' she said. It was now that she gained her reputation for eccentricity. Being an outsider she would have got it anyway, but this precipitated matters.

'Oh, you like it, do you?' asked an elderly farmer, buying a quarter of boiled ham for his tea. 'Well, well, then.'

That seemed to sum it up . . .

Alice Thomas Ellis: Unexplained Laughter (1985)

A small war

Climbing from Merthyr through the dew of August mornings
When I was a centaur-cyclist, on the skills of wheels
I'd loop past The Storey Arms, past steaming lorries
Stopped for flasks of early tea, and fall into Breconshire.
A thin road under black Fan Frynych – which keeps its winter
Shillings long through spring – took me to the Senni valley.

That was my plenty, to rest on the narrow saddle
Looking down on the farms, letting the simple noises
Come singly up. It was there I saw a ring-ousel
Wearing the white gash of his mountains; but every
Sparrow's feather in that valley was rare, golden,
Perfect. It was an Eden fourteen miles from home.

Evan Drew, my second cousin, lived there. A long, slow man
With a brown gaze I remember him. From a hill farm
Somewhere on the slope above Heol Senni he sent his sons,
Boys a little older than I, to the Second World War.
They rode their ponies to the station, they waved
Goodbye, they circled the spitting sky above Europe.

I would not fight for Wales, the great battle-cries
Do not arouse me. I keep short boundaries holy,
Those my eyes have recognised and my heart has known
As welcome. Nor would I fight for her language. I spend
My few pence of Welsh to amuse my friends, to comment
On the weather. They carry no thought that could be mine.

It's the small wars I understand. So now that forty
People lock their gates in Senni, keeping the water out
With frailest barriers of love and anger. I'd fight for them.
Five miles of land, enough small farms to make a heaven,
Are easily trapped on the drawing-board, a decision
Of the pen drowns all, Yes, the great towns need

The humming water, yet, I have taken my rods to other
Swimming valleys and happily fished above the vanished
Field. I know the arguments. It is a handful of earth
I will not argue with, and the slow cattle swinging weightily
Home. When I open the taps in my English bathroom
I am surprised they do not run with Breconshire blood.

Leslie Norris

Border incident

Its churchy reverence for food, these waiters grave
amongst candles, made the place seem empty.
My waiter (André apparently) had passed
the collection plate while I sipped coffee, lingering.
To tip or not? The service had been quiet, fast;
short of loose change. I could always give a blessing.

They were being shown to the table next to mine
as I glanced up. Fiftyish, officer material, good school –
she was in charge, I thought. His was a bald front
of managerial class, a pink all-seeing lens,
as he rearranged his hands before him then sat blunt
at his polished desk, its line of silver pens.

André approached. 'Good evening, madam'. She bowed
as he passed the menu. 'Good evening, s . . . '.
He peered down, served him an eager stare.
'It's *you*, Mr Prys-Evans! How are you then?
How are things in Bont?' And he pulled up a chair.
Bald Prys-Evans froze, seemed to count a long slow ten

but 'Fine, Jack, fine,' replied at last. They chatted
awhile – Jack had left South Wales in '75, I learned –
while the wife's crisp skirt breathed rustling sighs.
As they ordered food, Jack scribbling in biro
on his open palm, I saw her close her eyes.
Three different kinds of wonder watched him go.

The main course came and went and I sat there
riveted. I'd learnt quite a lot about Bont by then,
about bank manager Prys-Evans too, whose steely
wife seemed about to close their joint account for good.
Nodding, he'd suffered all Jack's homesick bonhomie
as if about to explode, knowing he never would.

When they'd gone, as I was leaving at last,
'Nice to see folks from home,' I said to Jack.
'Aye, Prys-Evans rules the roost there'. He smiled.
'But I fixed his meal all right. See his face
all the time he was eating – drove him wild
I did! Bont. I can't stand the bloody place'.

John Davies

History

The Dream of Rhonabwy

In the collection of medieval stories The Mabinogion *the one concerning the dream of Rhonabwy is rooted in the area around Welshpool.*

Set during the time when Madawc ruled much of Powys, it begins with an account of a search for his missing brother Iorwerth. Iorwerth felt slighted by Madawc's possession of land and decided to resort to violent revenge by murder, destruction and the taking of prisoners.

One of the army of men under Madawc's command is Rhonabwy, and during the search for the villainous brother he and two other men seek refreshment at the home of Heilyr Goch, but are detained overnight by a fierce storm. Rhonabwy falls asleep on a yellow calf-skin and in a dream is transported to King Arthur's encampment on an island on the Severn.

As soon as sleep had come upon his eyes, it seemed to him that he was journeying with his companions across the plain of Argyngroeg, as he thought that he went towards Rhyd y Groes on the Severn. As he journeyed, he heard a mighty noise, the like whereof heard he never before; and looking behind him, he beheld a youth with yellow curling hair, and with his beard newly trimmed, mounted on a chestnut horse, whereof the legs were grey from the top of the forelegs, and from the bend of the hindlegs downwards. And the rider wore a coat of yellow satin sewn with green silk, and on his thigh was a gold-hilted sword, with a scabbard of new leather of Cordova, belted with the skin of the deer, and clasped with gold. And over this was a scarf of yellow satin wrought with green silk, the borders whereof were likewise green. And the green of the caparison of the horse, and of his rider, was as green as the leaves of the fir-tree, and the yellow was as yellow as the blossom of the broom. So fierce as the aspect of the night, that fear seized upon them, and they began to flee. And the knight pursued them. And when the horse breathed forth, the men became distant from him, and when he drew in his breath, they were drawn near to him, even to the horse's chest. And when he had overtaken them, they besought his mercy. 'You have it gladly,' said he; 'fear nought'. 'Ha, chieftain, since thou hast mercy upon me, tell me also who thou art,' said Rhonabwy. 'I will not conceal my lineage from thee; but by my nickname am I best known.' 'And wilt thou tell us what thy nickname is?' 'I will tell you; it is Iddawc Cordd Prydain.' 'Ha, chieftain,' said Rhonabwy, 'why art thou called thus?' 'I will tell thee. I was one of the messengers between Arthur and Medrawd his nephew, at the battle of Camlan; and I was then a reckless youth, and through my desire for battle, I kindled strife between them, and stirred up wrath, when I was sent by Arthur the Emperor to reason with Medrawd, and to show him, that he was his foster-father and his uncle, and to seek for peace, lest the sons of the Kings of the Island of Britain, and of the nobles, should be slain. And whereas Arthur charged me with the fairest sayings he could think of, I uttered unto Medrawd the harshest I could devise. And therefore am I called Iddawc Cordd Prydain, for from this did the battle of Camlan ensue. And three nights before the end of the battle of Camlan I left them, and went to the Llech Las in North Britain to do penance. And there I remained doing penance seven years, and after that I gained pardon.'

Then lo! they heard a mighty sound which was much louder than that which they had heard before, and when they looked round towards the sound, they beheld a ruddy youth, without beard or whiskers, noble of mien, and mounted on a stately courser. And from the shoulders and the front of the knees downwards the horse was bay. And upon the man was a dress of red satin wrought with yellow silk, and yellow were the borders of his scarf. And such parts of his apparel and of the trappings of his horse as were yellow, as yellow were they as the blossom of the broom, and such as were red, were as ruddy as the ruddiest blood in the world.

Then, behold the horseman overtook them, and he asked of Iddawc, a share of the little men that were with him. 'That which is fitting for me to grant I will grant, and thou shalt be a companion to them as I have been.' And the horseman went away. 'Iddawc,' inquired Rhonabwy, 'who was that horseman?' 'Rhuvawn Pebyr the son of Prince Deorthach.'

And they journeyed over the plain of Argyngroeg as far as the ford of Rhyd y Groes on the Severn. And for a mile around the ford on both sides of the road, they saw tents and encampments, and there was the clamour of a mighty host. And they came to the edge of the ford, and there they beheld Arthur sitting on a flat island below the ford.

The Mabinogion, translated by Lady Charlotte Guest

The Last Stand of Caractacus

The western tribes of Britain campaigned bravely against the encroachment of Roman colonisation and Caractacus (Caradoc in Welsh) became the warrior leader of the Ordovices, the tribe who lived in North Wales and the northern border region at that time.

As the Romans were moving south against him he tried to reach his hill fort near what is now Church Stretton – the hill is now known as Caer Caradoc – in order to mastermind his campaign. But he was forced to retreat to another of his forts, between Clun and Knighton, and it was here in 57 AD that the Romans attacked. The Ordovices were outnumbered and outmanoeuvred and following the battle Caractacus' wife and children were captured and taken prisoner. Caractacus himself fled north but was betrayed by another tribe and he also fell into enemy hands. He was then taken to Rome and appeared before Claudius.

This major event in borderland history is related by the Roman writer Tacitus.

The natural ferocity of the inhabitants was intensified by their belief in the prowess of Caractacus, whose many undefeated battles – and even many victories – had made him pre-eminent among British chieftains. His deficiency in strength was compensated by superior cunning and topographical knowledge. Transferring the war to the country of the Ordovices, he was joined by everyone who found the prospect of a Roman peace alarming. Then Caractacus staked his fate on a battle. He selected a site where numerous factors – notably approaches and escape-routes – helped him and impeded us. On one side there were steep hills. Wherever the gradient was gentler, stones were piled into a kind of rampart. And at his front there was a river without easy crossings. The defences were strongly manned.

The British chieftains went round their men, encouraging and heartening them to be unafraid and optimistic, and offering other stimulants to battle. Caractacus, as he hastened to one point and another, stressed that this was the day, this the battle, which would either win back their freedom or enslave them for ever. He invoked their ancestors, who by routing Julius Caesar had valorously preserved their present descendants from Roman officials and taxes – and their wives and children from defilement. These exhortations were applauded. Then every man swore by his tribal oath that no enemy weapons would make them yield – and no wounds either.

This eagerness dismayed the Roman commander disconcerted as he already was by the river-barrier, the fortifications supplementing it, the overhanging cliffs, and the ferocious crowds of defenders at every point. But our soldiers shouted for battle, clamouring that courage could overcome everything; and their colonels spoke to the same effect, to encourage them further.

After a reconnaissance to detect vulnerable and invulnerable points, Ostorious led his enthusiastic soldiers forward. They crossed the river without difficulty, and reached the rampart. But then, in an exchange of missiles, they came off worse in wounds and casualties. However, under a roof of locked shields, the Romans demolished the crude and clumsy stone embankment, and in the subsequent fight at close quarters the natives were driven to the hill-tops. Our troops pursued them closely. While light-armed auxiliaries attacked with javelins, the heavy regular infantry advanced in close formation. The British, unprotected by breastplates or helmets, were thrown into disorder. If they stood up to the auxiliaries they were cut down by the swords and spears of the regulars, and if they faced the latter they succumbed to the auxiliaries' broadswords and pikes. It was a great victory. Caractacus' wife and daughter were captured: his brother surrendered. He himself sought sanctuary with Cartimandua, queen of the Brigantes. But the defeated have no refuge. He was arrested, and handed over to the conquerors.

The war in Britain was in its ninth year. The reputation of Caractacus had spread beyond the islands and through the neighbouring provinces to Italy itself. These people were curious to see the man who had defied our power for so many years. Even at Rome his name meant something! Besides, the emperor's attempts to glorify himself conferred additional glory on Caractacus in defeat. For the people were summoned as though for a fine spectacle, while the Guard stood in arms on the parade ground before their camp. Then there was a march past, with Caractacus' petty vassals, and the decorations and neckchains and spoils of his foreign wars. Next were displayed his brothers, wife and daughter. Last came the king himself. The others, frightened, degraded themselves by entreaties. But there were no downcast looks or appeals for mercy from Caractacus. On reaching the dais he spoke in these terms.

'Had my lineage and rank been accompanied by only moderate success, I should have come to this city as friend rather than prisoner, and you would not have disdained to ally yourself peacefully with one so nobly born, the ruler of so many nations. As it is, humiliation is my lot, glory yours. I had horses, men, arms, wealth. Are you surprised I am sorry to lose them? If you want to rule the world, does it follow that everyone else welcomes enslavement? If I had surrendered without a blow before being brought before you, neither my downfall nor your triumph would have become famous. If you execute me, they will be forgotten. Spare me, and I shall be an everlasting token of your mercy!'

Claudius responded by pardoning him and his wife and brothers.

Tacitus (AD c.55 – c.117): 'The Annals of Ancient Rome', translated by Michael Grant

Beacons

They saw him in the winter afternoon
The lone horseman stepping up the high hill,
Hoofs placed delicately as the light failed,
His cloak fighting the wind off the dry scree.
Two centuries ago they saw him, leaving
The old Brecon road, climbing on tussocks,
Picking a practised way through the sheep tracks,
Coarse grass and peat bog to the mountain top.

There, with tinder box, he crouched over sticks,
Pitch, and timbers at the cairn, catching flame
From Pembroke, Gloucester, or Hereford hills.
He served this ancient secular altar,
Priest of the high and country tower, unbound
By language, at the very eye of Wales.

So far he tops my thought that it may seem
As if he stands there yet, chafing away
And chipping for a flame to crown the hill –
In my mind's eye, Horatio, in my

Mind's eye – absurdly out of date, as if
Solemnly playing some druidical
Ritual piously preserved against
The muddy flux of change across the Dyke.

Cry aloud, prophet, for perhaps their god
In England is travelling, or asleep.
Expect no spark to fall from heaven. You must
Grind out your own flame, fire your Welsh beacon
To cry danger to Stoke and Birmingham.
Clean fire to dirty fires, woodsmoke to soot.

Bryan Morris (1930-2002)

Haunted Country

The Welsh border, where Wales and England meet, is haunted country. There are misty hills and secret valleys, dark ridges whose slopes are trodden only by sheep and their lonely shepherds. In this landscape there have been whispered stories of strange happenings, of wizards and spells, of changelings, disappearances. Some of these stories have been written down and some have not.

Welshpool is full of stories that have never been written down – till now. They have been passed on by whisper, from generation to generation. Even today the people of Welshpool do not tell such stories aloud, and they never tell them to strangers. They have heard of strangers who come and go, appear and vanish.

And the word they whisper most of all is 'castle'. Welshpool is a small town that sprawls on a hillside. Half-way up that hill you can turn off along a side lane that leads to great wrought-iron gates. Beyond, through the innocent-seeming meadows with the pools and shining buttercups, runs the back way to a castle – Powis Castle. And it is there that the magic gathers. It gathers, coils itself up like a spring and is released – in mist.

Helen Cresswell: 'Stonestruck' (1995)

Guilty

Amwythig, Henffordd and Caer are Shrewsbury, Hereford and Chester.
Graham Davies wrote the poem as a response to A.E. Houseman's 'The Welsh Marches'.

The border towns are black and white
and peaceful seeming to the sight,
although the stones below the mud
are stained dark red with blood.

In border towns which violence built
there's commerce now of *Sais* and Celt,
false fair-day friends who sell and buy
in *Amwythig, Henffordd, Caer.*

You guilty cities, hear this song:
the stones recall the ancient wrong,
so let your prayers be lifted high,
Amwythig, Henffordd, Caer.

Grahame Davies, translated by the poet.

Tretower Court

Tretower Court is a well-preserved fourteenth century manor house near Crickhowell (Crucywel). Between the fifteenth and the eighteenth centuries it was the home of the Vaughan family. The family crest consisted of an image of three children with snakes around their necks.

The place is still haunted by three fair-haired children
with snakes coiled round their necks. Sheep are scattered like daisies
near the bird-infested tower.
Light flows through what was the roof.

They go in and out
of the empty gallery rooms, always one door ahead of you.
Some day you'll surprise one who squints at the shining fields
and writes like Henry Vaughan.

Merryn Williams

Continuity and Persistence

Everywhere we see how the county's history has been dictated by its geography and its climate. The ranges from Pumlumon up to Moel Sych in the Berwyn Mountains effectively divide the county into two parts. On the west, the rivers have only a short journey before they reach the sea, the land is high and rocky and villages more isolated; here the Welsh language and traditions are more persistent than in the east near the English border, although even there it is surprising how the old customs have lingered on. 'Continuity and persistence are remarkable features of the life of Wales.' One is constantly finding reminders of this in local tales, in place-names, in still living traditions. It is possible to hear a Welshman talking affectionately of some figure of the past as if he had been a close acquaintance, and had only in the last month or so been carried to the churchyard. 'It was in that field there that it happened. They had an argument, you see, about the boundaries, and he picked up his bill-hook and he struck the man and killed him.' The listener, enthralled by the dramatic narrative, wonders if he can read the details in the *County Times*, only to discover that it all happened two hundred years ago. The past is still alive and interesting and part of present day living.

Pauline Phillips: A View of Montgomeryshire: 1977

Llywarch Hen

. . . it may not be amiss, cursorily to acquaint the reader, that Llywarch Hen was a prince of the North of England, in the sixth century. He had been always active, though unfortunately, in opposing the encroachments of the Northumbrian Saxons; in which contest he lost his patrimonial territories, and the greater number of his four-and-twenty sons; with the remainder he fled thence, and took refuge under the hospitable roof of Cynddylan, Prince of Powys, who had his residence at or near Shrewsbury, after whose defeat and death, our bard, worn out with age and misery, retired into the wilds of Powysland, where he sank under his misfortunes, being about 150 years old.

Walter Davies: The English Works of Walter Davies (Gwallter Mechain), edited by Silvan Evans

Cynddylan's Hall

The English are invading the good land of Powys. By the time this sequence starts, they have killed Cynddylan and destroyed his home. Heledd is lamenting over the ruins. Elfan, Caeawg (if that is indeed a proper name, and not some epithet describing Cynddylan), Cynon, Gwiawn and Gwyn, whom she mentions, are presumably her brothers, the sons of Cyndrwyn.

Dark is Cynddylan's hall tonight
  With no fire, no bed.
I weep awhile, then am silent.

Dark is Cynddylan's hall tonight
  With no fire, no candle.
Save for God, who'll keep me sane?

Dark is Cynddylan's hall tonight
  With no fire, no light.
Grieving for you overcomes me.

Dark of roof is Cynddylan's hall
  After that blest assembly.
Woe who neglects the good that offers!

Cynddylan's hall, you've gone uncomely,
  Your shield is in the grave.
While he lived, doors needed no bar.

Forlorn is Cynddylan's hall tonight
  For the man that owned it.
O for death, why did it leave me?

No ease in Cynddylan's hall tonight
  On the top of hard rock
With no lord, or retinue, or prowess!

Dark is Cynddylan's hall tonight
  With no fire, no songs.
My cheek's worn out with tears.

It wounds me to see Cynddylan's hall
With no roof, no fire,
Dead is my lord; I yet live.

Waste is Cynddylan's hall tonight
After strong warriors,
Elfan, Cynddylan, Caeawg.

Desolate is Cynddylan's hall tonight
After the respect I had,
With no men, no women to care for it.

Quiet is Cynddylan's hall tonight,
Now it has lost its lord.
Merciful God, what shall I do?

Dark of roof is Cynddylan's hall
After the English destroyed
Cynddylan and Elfan of Powys.

Dark is Cynddylan's hall tonight
For the seed of Cyndrwyn,
Cynon and Gwiawn and Gwyn.

Hour upon hour, Cynddylan's hall wounds me
After the great conversing
That I watched on your hearth.

Anonymous, translated by Tony Conran

Llywelyn ab Madog

Llywelyn, son of Madog ap Meredydd, prince of Powys, was a
young chieftain of great promise, but who was slain in 1159. He is
styled 'the only hope of all the men of Powys'. The *Myv. Arch.*
contains Englynion in his praise (attributed to Llywarch Llaety, but
which, according to both Stephens and Price, were more probably
written by Llywarch Llew Cad), reckoned by Stephens among 'the
most interesting pieces of the twelfth century'.

'In the whole range of our literature, we have not as lively a portrait of a chieftain; the minutest features are noticed, without the *tout d'ensemble* being lost sight of, and Llywelyn ab Madog stands as palpable before us, as if his portrait had been painted on the canvas. In the easy flow of the language, the minuteness of the description, and the spirit of the whole delineation, we have a collection of merits nor frequently to be met with in the works of the bards, and the prince described seems so deserving of being the idol of a poet's fancy, that the poet and his subject share an unbounded admiration.'

The poem opens with the question –

'Gofynnwys nebun ny raen gan rei &c.'

The following is a translation of the first twelve stanzas:-

Does no one ask, – are men so unconcerned
Before unsheathing their swords,
Who is yon mail-clad youth?
Who is the haughty warrior before us?

A glorious prince full of intelligence,
None will be allowed to lead him,
He is a prince, valiant, powerful and war-loving,
Llywelyn the enemy of Gwynedd.

Whose swift moving shield is that,
And bright shining spear?
Who is the determined warlike chief,
Who holds it by its armlets?

It is the shield of Llywelyn the brave
Protector of his country's rights;
A shield with a man's shoulder behind it;
A shield which carries terror before it.

Whose is the flashing sword which cuts the air,
A sure wound-inflictor;
An emblem of honour it will be,
And in that right hand will destroy enemies.

He who handles it is the defender of his country,
Renowned for downward strokes;
A courageous soldier in the day of battle,
Is the hero of Mechain, – his country's pride.

Whose is that red helmet of battle
Surmounted with a fierce wolf?
Who is the rider of the fierce white steed?
What is his name? how wonderful his appearance!

He is called long-handed Llywelyn,
The irresistible leader of conflict,
Commander of men of the terrible shout,
Devastator of England; faultless and perfect is he.

Whose is the suit of complete armour?
He will not fly from the battle field.
Who is this hero of princely race?
I ask you all, whence sprang he?

He is a renowned and valiant prince,
Famed for bravery and slaughtering;
The majestic Chief, dreadful in the fight,
Is the son of Madog ab Meredydd.

Whose is the war-steed, fastest in the race,
Which so haughtily paws the ground?
Who the prince so loved by his army,
With the spear which pierces without warning?

He is a known, ambitious chief,
Who, as long as God supports him,
Will be famed as conqueror, brave and glorious –
Worthy of the men of Tysiliaw.

Richard Williams: Montgomeryshire Worthies (1894)

The Siege of Pains Castle

The castles in Radnorshire are in utter ruin, yet they were notable structures.

Pains Castle is a complete wreck. It was built by Paganus FitzJohn in the reign of Henry I. A legendary tale is connected with it. William de Braos and his attendants were out hunting when they saw a beautiful girl with her attendants disporting themselves on the lake Bwch Llyn, about two miles from Pains Castle, and he at once with his men carried off the damsel to his castle. She was of royal Welsh race, and her kinsfolk sought for her in vain, but suspected that the brutal Norman baron had taken her away. They appealed to Rhys ab Gruffydd, the prince, and he demanded her release. De Braos pretended that he was slandered, that he was guiltless in the matter, and that he knew not where she was. However, the girl made signals by means of a candle in her window. And Rhys, now convinced that she was there, gathered a large force, attacked the castle, and De Braos, unable to hold out, was forced to surrender the lady.

There is a certain amount of foundation for the story. Rhys did attack Pains Castle, and brought De Braos to terms; but we do not know that any lady was mixed up in the facts of the story. However a later Rhys ab Maredudd, in the time of Edward I, did capture one of the royal castles and left his wife there whilst he pursued his ravages. But the English drove him back, and it was only by means of a clever ruse that he was able to get his wife out of the castle and take her away with him. It was then, doubtless, that the signals with the candle were made. There years after Rhys ab Gruffydd had attacked Pains Castle, it was besieged by Gwenwynwyn, Prince of Powys, but after lying before it three weeks, he retired without having succeeded. It is this siege that has been made use of by Sir Walter Scott in his novel *The Betrothed*.

S. Baring Gould (1834-1924): A Book of South Wales

Born Invulnerable

The river, whose stream washes on three sides the base of the proud eminence on which the castle is situated, curves away from the fortress and its corresponding village on the west, and the hill sinks downward to an extensive plain, so extremely level as to indicate its alluvial origin. Lower down, at the extremity of this plain, where the banks again close on the river, were situated the manufacturing houses of the stout Flemings, which were now burning in a bright flame. The bridge, a high, narrow combination of arches of unequal size, was about half-a-mile distant from the castle, in the very centre of the plain. The river itself ran in a deep rocky channel, was often unfordable, and at all times difficult of passage, giving considerable advantage to the defenders of the castle, who had spent on other occasions many a dear drop of blood to defend the pass, which Raymond Berenger's fantastic scruples now induced him to abandon. The Welshmen, seizing the opportunity with the avidity with which men grasp an unexpected benefit, were fast crowding over the high and steep arches, while new bands, collecting from different points upon the farther bank, increased the continued stream of warriors, who, passing leisurely and uninterrupted, formed their line of battle on the plain opposite to the castle.

At first Father Aldrovand viewed their motions without anxiety, nay, with the scornful smile of one who observes an enemy in the act of falling into the snare spread for them by superior skill. Raymond Berenger, with his little body of infantry and cavalry, were drawn up on the easy hill which is betwixt the castle and the plain, ascending from the former towards the fortress; and it seemed clear to the Dominican, who had not entirely forgotten in the cloister his ancient military experience, that it was the Knight's purpose to attack the disordered enemy when a certain number had crossed the river, and the others were partly on the farther side, and partly engaged in the slow and perilous manoeuvre of effecting their passage. But when large bodies of the white-mantled Welshmen were permitted without interruption to take such order on the plain as their habits of fighting recommended, the monk's countenance, though he still endeavoured to speak encouragement to the terrified Eveline, assumed a different and an anxious expression; and his acquired habits of resignation contended strenuously with his ancient military ardour. 'Be patient,' he said, 'my daughter, and be of good comfort; thine eyes shall behold the dismay of yonder barbarous enemy. Let but a minute elapse, and thou shalt see them scattered like dust – Saint George! they will surely cry thy name now, or never!'

The monk's beads passed meanwhile rapidly through his hands, but many an expression of military impatience mingled itself with his orisons. He could not conceive the cause why each successive throng of mountaineers, led under their different banners, and headed by their respective chieftains, was permitted, without interruption, to pass the difficult defile, and extend themselves in battle array on the near side of the bridge, while the English, or rather Anglo-Norman cavalry, remained stationary, without so much as laying their lances in rest. There remained, as he thought, but one hope – one only rational explanation of this unaccountable inactivity – this voluntary surrender of every advantage of ground, when that of numbers was so tremendously on the side of the enemy. Father Aldrovand concluded that the succours of the Constable of Chester, and other Lord Marchers, must be in the immediate vicinity, and that the Welsh were only permitted to pass the river without opposition, that their retreat might be the more effectually cut off, and their defeat, with a deep river in their rear, rendered the more signally calamitous. But even while he clung to this hope, the monk's heart sank within him, as, looking in every direction from which the expected succours might arrive, he could neither see nor hear the slightest token which announced their approach. In a frame of mind approaching more nearly to despair than to hope, the old man continued alternately to tell his beads, to gaze anxiously around, and to address some words of consolation in broken phrases to the young lady, until the general shout of the Welsh, ringing from the river to the battlements of the castle, warned him, in a note of exultation, that the very last of the British had defiled through the pass, and that their whole formidable array stood prompt for action upon the hither side of the river.

This thrilling and astounding clamour, to which each Welshman lent his voice with all the energy of defiance, thirst of battle, and hope of conquest, was at length answered by the blast of the Norman trumpets, – the first sign of activity which had been exhibited on the part of Raymond Berenger. But cheerily as they rang, the trumpets, in comparison of the shout which they answered, sounded like the silver whistle of the stout boatswain amid the howling of the tempest.

At the same moment when the trumpets were blown, Berenger gave signal to the archers to discharge their arrows, and the men-at-arms to advance under a hail-storm of shafts, javelins, and stones, shot, darted, and slung by the Welsh against their steel-clad assailants.

The veterans of Raymond, on the other hand, stimulated by so many victorious recollections, confident in the talents of their accomplished leader, and undismayed even by the desperation of their circumstances, charged the mass of the Welshmen with their usual determined valour. It was a gallant sight to see this little body of cavalry advance to the onset, their plumes floating above their helmets, their lances in rest, and projecting six feet in length before the breasts of their courses; their shields hanging from their necks, that their left hands might have freedom to guide their horses; and the whole body rushing on with an equal front, and a momentum of speed which increased with every second. Such an onset might have startled naked men (for such were the Welsh, in respect of the mail-sheathed Normans), but it brought no terrors to the ancient British, who had long made it their boast that they exposed their bare bosoms and white tunics to the lances and swords of the men-at-arms, with as much confidence as if they had been born invulnerable.

Walter Scott (1771-1832): The Betrothed

An Oasis

. . . arriving at Machynlleth out of its wooded hills is like arriving at an oasis, or a haven. On its sheltered green plateau beside the river, the place has an air of safety very welcome to the medieval traveller. Outcrops of high ground command the town. On the hill to the north, Gallt y Gog, the tumbled fortifications of the Stone Age people are still useful works of defence. On Yr Wylfa, the Watchplace, to the south, the remains of a Roman fort make a strongpoint still, and a few miles downstream another Roman work guards the estuary. Amidst all the squalors and dangers of medievalism people feel instinctively safe in Machynlleth – even the irrepressible Vikings never came up this river, and the town prospers by its security. The Wednesday market draws buyers and sellers from many miles around, the inns and taverns are famous. The streets are lively always with Welsh mule and wagon trains arriving on the coastal roads, English traders and functionaries coming from Newtown, Montgomery, Welshpool and Amwythig over the border – Shrewsbury to the English.

At one end of town the Maen Llwyd stands undisturbed on its tufty common, a holy object still after so many years of Christianity. At the other end of town the parish church of St Peter stands within the circular enclosure of a vanished Celtic church, long ago associated with the cult of St Cybi. Between these two shrines the little market town compactly huddles, home to no more than a couple of hundred people, but always busy with visitors and travellers. Beside the wide and muddy main thoroughfare, Heol Maen-gwyn, two white quartz boulders stand as talismans: the street runs westward from the common and is lined with houses and shops, some thatched, some tiled, some built of rough uncut stones, some of mud and wattle, and one at least, Tŷ Mawr half-way down the street, grand enough to have two floors, glass windows and a stable yard. A market cross marks the junction of Heol Maen-gwyn with the coastal roads, which run away southward to the river quays of Derwen-las, northward to the ford over the Dyfi, the most famous river crossing in Wales.

Jan Morris and Twm Morys: A Machynlleth Triad (1993)

A Thoroughly Welsh Town

Machynlleth, pronounced Machynlleth, is one of the principal towns of the district which the English call Montgomeryshire, and the Welsh Shire Trefaldwyn or the Shire of Baldwin's town, Trefaldwyn or the town of Baldwin being the Welsh name for the town which is generally termed Montgomery. It is situated in nearly the centre of the valley of the Dyfi amidst pleasant green meadows, having to the north the river, from which, however, it is separated by a gentle hill. It possesses a stately church, parts of which are of considerable antiquity, and one or two good streets. It is a thoroughly Welsh town, and the inhabitants, who amount in number to about four thousand, speak the ancient British language with considerable purity.

Machynlleth has been the scene of remarkable events and is connected with remarkable names, some of which have rung through the world. At Machynlleth in 1402 Owain Glyndŵr, after several brilliant victories over the English, held a parliament in a house which is yet to be seen in the Eastern Street, and was formally crowned King of Wales; in his retinue was the venerable bard Iolo Goch, who imagining that he now saw the old prophecy fulfilled, namely that a prince of the race of Cadwaladr should rule the Britons, after emancipating them from the Saxon yoke, greeted the chieftain with an ode.

George Borrow (1803-1881): Wild Wales

Owain Glyndŵr's Court

I have promised twice before now,
fair promise, promising a journey;
let everyone fulfill, as much as is due,
his promise which he promises.
A very great pilgrimage,
certain prosperity, such a clear destination,
is going, swift promise,
it is beneficial, towards Owain's court;
swiftly will I go there,
not bad, there will I dwell

to bring honour into my life
by exchanging greetings with him;
my liege can, highest lineage,
bright golden head, receive an old codger;
is it praiseworthy, though it be but alms,
course without shame, to be kind to the old.
I will go to his court in haste,
the most splendid of the two hundred;
a baron's court, place of refinement,
where many poets come, place of the good life;
queen of great Powys, Maig's land,
promise of good hope.

This is its manner and its form
in a bright circle of water within an embankment:
(isn't the court fine?) a bridge on the lake,
and one gate through which would go a hundred loads;
there are couples, they are couple work,
every couple is coupled together;
Patrick's bellhouse, French fruit,
the cloister of Westminster, comfortable enclosure;
each corner is bound together in the same way,
golden chancel, it is entirely symmetrical;
bonds side by side above,
cheek-to-cheek like an earthhouse,
and every one looking like a tight knot
is tied fast to the next one;
nine-plated buildings on the scale of eighteen mansions,
fair wooden buildings on top of a green hill;
on four wonderful pillars
his court is nearer to heaven;
on top of each stout wooden pillar
a loft built firmly on the summit of a croft,
and the four lofts of loveliness
coupled together where poets sleep;
the four bright lofts turned,
a very fair nest load, into eight lofts;
a tiled roof on every house with frowning forehead,
and a chimney from which the smoke would grow;
nine symmetrical identical halls,

and nine wardrobes by each one,
bright fair shops with fine contents,
a lovely full shop like London's Cheapside;
a cross-shaped church with a fair chalk-coloured exterior,
chapels with splendid glass windows;
a full bakehouse on every side of the court,
an orchard, a vineyard by a white court;
a lovely mill on flowing water,
and his dovecot with bright stone tower;
a fishpond, hollow enclosure,
what is needed to cast nets;
place most abounding, not for dispute,
in pike and fine sewin,
and his bord-land and his live birds,
peacocks, splendid herons;
bright meadows of grass and hay,
corn in well-kept fields,
the rabbit park of our patriarch,
ploughs and sturdy horses, great words;
by the court, outshining the other,
stags graze in another park;
his serfs perform all fitting tasks,
those are the necessities of an estate,
bringing the best brew of beer from Shrewsbury,
liquors of foaming bragget,
every drink, white bread and wine,
and his meat and his fire for his kitchen;
shelter of poets, everyone wherever he be,
were it daily, he will have everyone there –

Iolo Goch: translated by Dafydd Johnson

Sycharth

Owain Glyndŵr's hill or mount at Sycharth, unlike the one bearing
his name on the banks of the Dee, is not an artificial hill, but the
work of nature, save and except that to a certain extent it has been
modified by the hand of man. It is somewhat conical and consists
of two steps or gradations, where two fosses scooped out of the hill

go round it, one above the other, the lower one embracing considerably the most space. Both these fosses are about six feet deep, and at one time doubtless were bricked, as stout large, red bricks are yet to be seen, here and there, in their sides. When I visited it it was covered with grass, but had once been subjected to the plough as various furrows indicated. The monticle stands not far from the western extremity of the valley, nearly midway between two hills which confront each other north and south, the one to the south being the hill which I had descended, and the other a beautiful wooded height which is called in the parlance of the country Llwyn Sycharth or the grove of Sycharth, from which comes the little gush of water which I had crossed, and which now turns the wheel of the factory and once turned that of Owain Glyndŵr's mill, and filled his two moats, part of the water by some mechanical means having been forced up the eminence. On the top of this hill or monticle in a timber house dwelt the great Welshman Owain Glyndŵr, with his wife, a comely, kindly woman, and his progeny, consisting of stout boys and blooming girls, and there, though wonderfully cramped for want of room, he feasted bards who requited his hospitality with alliterative odes very difficult to compose, and which at the present day only a few bookworms understand. There he dwelt for many years, the virtual if not the nominal king of North Wales, occasionally no doubt looking down with self-complaisance from the top of his fastness on the parks and fish-ponds of which he had several; his mill, his pigeon tower, his ploughed lands, and the cottages of a thousand retainers, huddled round the lower part of the hill, or strewn about the valley; and there he might have lived and died had not events caused him to draw the sword and engage in a war, at the termination of which Sycharth was a fire-scathed ruin, and himself a broken-hearted old man in anchorite's weeds, living in a cave on the estate of Sir John Scudamore, the great Herefordshire proprietor, who married his daughter Elen, his only surviving child.

George Borrow (1803-1881): 'Wild Wales'

A meeting on Long Mountain

After leaving Mathafarn on the morning of 12 August, Henry
Tudor probably marched northwards to Mallwyd and then east
through the pass of Bwlch-y-Fedwen to Castle Caereinon. Here,
where he was within striking distance of the upper Severn valley,
he spent the night of 12 August, according to tradition, at the
house of Dolarddun. But a subsidiary force may have marched
south-eastwards from Mathafarn to link with Rhys ap Thomas's
scouts in the vicinity of Newtown.

The following day, 13 August, after spending the previous
night at Dolarddun, Henry advanced six miles to Welshpool. He
then went to Long Mountain (Cefn Digoll) which overlooks the
Severn opposite Welshpool.

Here Henry met Rhys ap Thomas who 'with a great bande of
soldiers and with assuryd promises of loyalty yielded himself to
this protection' (Polydore Vergil). Other Welsh contingents from
north and north-east Wales also met Henry at Long Mountain.
These included the followers of William Griffith of Penrhyn (near
Bangor) and of Richard ap Howell of Mostyn in Flint. Another
prominent supporter of Henry from the north was Rhys Fawr ap
Meredudd of Plas Iolyn in the upper Conwy valley.

David Rees: The Son of Prophecy (1985)

A Just Man

My father was Richard Herbert, Esq., son of Edward Herbert, Esq.,
and grandchild to Sir Richard Herbert, Knight, who was a younger
son to Sir Richard Herbert, of Colebrook, in Monmouthshire, of all
whom I shall say a little. And first of my father, whom I remember
to have been black-haired and bearded, as all my ancestors of his
side are said to have been, of a manly or somewhat stern look, but
withal very handsome and well compact in his limbs, and of a
great courage, whereof he gave proof, when he was so barbarously
assaulted by many men in the churchyard at Llanerfyl, at what
time he would have apprehended a man who denied to appear to
justice; for, defending himself against them all, by the help only of
one John ap Howell Corbet, he chased his adversaries until a

124

villain, coming behind him, did over the shoulders of others wound him on the head behind with a forest bill until he fell down, though recovering himself again, notwithstanding his skull was cut through to the *pia mater* of the brain, he saw his adversaries fly away, and after walked home to his house at Llyssyn, where, after he was cured, he offered a single combat to the chief of the family, by whose procurement it was thought the mischief was committed; but he disclaiming wholly the action as not done by his consent, which he offered to testify by oath, and the villain himself flying into Ireland, whence he never returned, my father desisted from prosecuting the business any farther in that kind, and attained, not withstanding the said hurt, that health and strength, that he returned to his former exercises in a country life, and became the father of many children. As for his integrity in his places of deputy-lieutenant of the county, justice of the peace, and *custos rotulorum*, which he, as my grandfather before him, held, it is so memorable to this day, that it was said his enemies appealed to him for justice, which they also found on all occasions.

Lord Edward Herbert (1583-1648): Autobiography

An Abortive Plot

The famous or infamous Sir David Gam belonged to an estated and important family in Brecon. His house was at Newton, near the town, and he claimed descent from Caradog Freichfras, one of the knights of King Arthur's Round Table, Lord of Gloucester, Cornwall, and Brecon. Sir David's father's name was Llewelyn, and Gam was a nickname given to David because he squinted. In the English camp, where he served under Henry V, he would have been known as ap Llewelyn, and this with Shakespeare has become Flewellin. In 1402 he formed an iniquitous plot to assassinate Owain Glyndŵr, when that great man had summoned a Welsh parliament to meet at Machynlleth. The plot was disclosed, and Glyndŵr consigned David Gam to prison, but afterwards released him (1412), when he took a solemn oath not to bear arms, or otherwise to oppose the measures of Glyndŵr. But no sooner was he free than he used his liberty to violate in every way his oath. He betrayed the designs of the Welsh prince to

Henry whenever he learnt them, and he attacked Glyndŵr's partisans whenever he met them. Owain was so exasperated at his perfidy that he entered Brecknock and burnt Gam's house to the ground. After which, meeting one of David's tenants on the road, he tauntingly told him:-

'If a squinting red-haired knave
Meet thee, and perchance would crave
To know what fate his house befell,
Say that a cinder heap will tell.'

Shortly after, quarrelling with a kinsman in the street of Brecon, David killed him, and to escape prosecution, fled to England and attached himself to the Lancastrian party. He was with Henry V on the field of Agincourt, where he fell.

S. Baring-Gould (1834-1924): A Book of South Wales

A Devilish Woman

In the parish of Llanbister is the old mansion of Llwyn-went. Here in the fifteenth century was held a festive gathering, during which a quarrel arose between David Fychan and his cousin-german, John Hir, Long John, son of Philip Fychan, as to the extent of their respective estates. They fought with swords, and David was run through the body and killed. His sister Ellen, wife of Thomas ab Rosser Vaughan, of Hergest, resolved on avenging his death. Disguised as a man, she repaired to an archery meeting in the adjoining parish of Llanddewi Ystradenny, and challenged the best archer in the field. Long John accepted the challenge, and fixed his arrow in the centre of the target. He was followed by Ellen, who placed the arrow on the string, drew the bow to full stretch, and then, suddenly turning, sent it through the heart of John Hir. For this deed she earned the sobriquet of Gethin, or The Terrible. She is also spoken of as 'a devilish woman'.

S. Baring-Gould (1834-1924): A Book of South Wales

King of Powys

Heare lyeth the body of
John, ap Robert of Porth, ap
David, ap Griffydd, ap David Vaughan,
ap Blethyn, ap Griffydd, ap
Meredith, ap Iorwerth, ap Llewelyn, ap Ieroth,
ap Heilyn, ap Cowryd, ap Cadvan, ap
Alawgwa, ap Cadell, the
KING OF POWYS;
who departed this life the 20th day of March,
in the year of our Lord God 1643,
and of his age 95.

Inscription on a tomb at Llanrhaeadr yng Nghinmeirch, Dyffryn Clwyd

A Remarkable Welshman

William Jones of Dolhywel, Llangadfan (Gwilym Cadfan, 1726-95), conducted an ongoing correspondence with Walter Davies, and it was Davies who penned Jones's obituary for *The Cambrian Register* in 1796. However, Jones fitted into no circle; he was an isolated figure and one of the most remarkable Welshmen of his age. Apart from a brief period in one of Griffith Jones's circulating schools, this doughty tenant farmer was largely self-taught. Intellectual isolation continually blighted his efforts at self-advancement: 'it was my lot to be born, bred and confined in this obscure corner where I can but seldom enjoy the pleasure of conversing with men of knowledge', he observed towards the end of his life. Nevertheless, he mastered Latin and English, and he was one of the few Welshmen who had read Voltaire. He nurtured a curiosity about astronomy and medicine, and he was well regarded as a quack doctor in neighbouring communities. He was avid in his pursuit of the literary and cultural legacy of Wales, providing friends with details of folk songs and poetry and collecting the pedigrees of the Welsh nobility with a view to their publication. These interests, as he later recalled, were beset with difficulties: 'at Cyfronnydd in this county all the books and manuscripts were locked up in the bake house with a maid servant who was ordered to burn them all in the oven. At Melin-y-grug they were thrown into the river.' Straitened circumstances also curtailed his enthusiasm. In 1795 poverty prevented his purchase of Edwards Jones's *Musical and Poetical Relicks* (a volume to which he had himself contributed), and it was only the charity of well-meaning friends that enabled him to obtain his own copy.

Melvin Humphreys:
'The Crises of Community: Montgomeryshire' (1996)

Sir John Pryce

Sir John, while still in his thirties, found joy and discomfort with Mrs Eleanour Jones. This widow made Sir John bury his wives in the family vault before she consented to become his third, and to prevent any backsliding on his part after the wedding, she made him come and live in her home at Buckland in Breconshire.

The move from his Severnside home must have been a wrench for Sir John, who took with him to Buckland the organ he had presented to Newtown church. Six years later the death of the third Lady Pryce coincided with the notoriety of Bridget Bostock, a woman known as the Cheshire Pythoness, who was supposed to have miraculous powers of healing by means of her saliva. Sir John wrote a long and flattering letter to this woman, asking her aid to raise his wife from the dead, and sending his coach-and six with proper servants for her journey. Though the Pythoness is supposed to have accepted Sir John's invitation, nothing is known of whatever interview they may have had.

This man who was so preoccupied with marriage and mortality, was overtaken by the latter while courting a fourth wife, to whom he willed his entire estate, a document which was nullified through a prior settlement in favour of his son

The sixth baronet, though blind through an accident, rode to hounds, a long lead being attached from his bridle to that of his groom's horse. In this fashion master and servant took jumps, and are even said to have cleared the lane leading down to the lower Bryn. The baronet died in the King's Bench prison, and left his wife a shilling, on account of her infidelity to him during his time in jail.

Brian Waters: Severn Stream (1947)

Mining

An integral part of the mid Wales mining area was that of south-west Montgomeryshire. When Walter Davies wrote of it in 1813 the only mine worth noting was Dylife. There were other mines in being at that time but they were of little importance, and in fact Davies described the Plynlimon country as being 'the most unpromising of all ranges for mine adventurers at (that) time'. Some ore was being raised at Aberdaunant in the first years of the century but it was to be many years before this mine proved profitable. Later an aged Cornish miner known as Old Brown, who believed fervently in the richness of the Llanidloes district, spent a fortune at the Old Gwestyn and Geufron mines before dying destitute in 1848.

W.J. Lewis: Lead Mining in Wales (1967)

An address to Newtown

Oh what a blissful place! By Severn's Banks so fair
Happy the Inhabitants; and wholesome is thy Air,
Nine years long, since last I've seen thee fled
Ah! when departing, my Heart in grief has bled.
Thy lasses fair and thy young men as kind
Thy flannel fine and generous every mind
But now, tis now, I wonder most
I see thy Improvements, well can thy townsmen boast
To London great, in short by the canal
Thy flannel goes, as quick as one can tell,
And thence from there, the Flannel's quickly hurled
To every part of Britain, and its known world;
Thy gaslight bright, thy new built houses high,
They factories lofts, seem smiling on the sky
Newtown, Newtown is surely now thy name
Britannia whole is joyful of thy fame;
Adieu Welsh Pool, thy Market swift is falling
Newtown's New Market Halls is daily booming
Auspicious buildings, Wales' greatest grandeur
Cambria's masterpiece, Manufacturer's pleasure;

New Bank, New Church, New Halls of great renown
New houses, new Flannel, new gas in brave Newtown.
Go on and flourish, thy Markets ever bless
With flannel, full, of Money and success.

Robert Parry (1833)

Wool

The nineteenth century in Montgomeryshire was a period when flannel manufacturing became a factory industry, gaining in importance until 1840 and then gradually declining. It was the age of mechanization, an age when water power and later steam power was harnessed. The early part of the century saw the amassing of great wealth by dozens of flannel manufacturers, it saw a spectacular increase in the population of the county, it saw prosperity. The latter part of the century saw bankruptcy and poverty, it saw depopulation and industrial depression and the almost total eclipse of woollen manufacturing in Montgomeryshire.

The progress of the industry from the close of the eighteenth century to the mid-nineteenth century was marked by the adoption of a variety of new pieces of machinery. These technological developments had a marked effect not only on production but also on the social organization of the textile manufacturing districts.

J. Geraint Jenkins: The Welsh Woollen Industry

Samuel Roberts

Samuel Roberts, who was born at Llanbryn-mair, and was a minister, a writer and a radical.

He founded a magazine, Y Cronicl, which was extremely influential in the propagation of Nonconformist ideas.

He was a progressive and was, for example, deeply opposed to the intervention of the state of education, and was therefore very critical of the report of the Blue Books commissioners.

His interests and concerns were not confined to Wales, however.

A debate arose in the mid nineteenth century which concerned Baron Rothschild, a Jew. Opinion was divided as to whether or not he should be allowed to take his seat in Parliament, partly because he wished to state his allegiance on a copy of the Old Testament rather than on the New Testament. The fact that he elected for a city of London seat seemed to carry little weight. In fact it was two years after Samuel Roberts' article that Rothschild achieved his objective.

Lord John Russell and the Government could establish a law in a few minutes to make the way completely clear for the Baron to take his place in Parliament immediately following his election. The Baron is completely content to take the vows upon the Old Testament, and he testifies solemnly that that is the most effective method for his conscience; and it is truly disgraceful that Lord John Russell and Sir Robert Harry Inglis and their friends are wasting so much of the valuable time of the country and Parliament, to boast their Christianity and their conscience and to bicker like fools and argue stubbornly about such a case.

Baron Rothschild is far more honest, and magnanimous, and conscientious, than they have ever been, and it is an everlasting shame to our country that the Baron, after having been elected for such a long time for the city of London, should be shut out of Parliament. He was elected more than once by the same people who elected Lord John. It is as fair for the sons of Abraham to have a voice in Parliament as it is for the sons of Omer, and the bastards of Hengist. Eternal shame on Lord Russell that he should quibble minutely and fake sighs instead of undoing the lock of captivity, and letting his rich and co-elected compatriot come in to join him in the court of Parliament. We have heard that some of the Parsons of the Church of England in Wales have sent petitions to Parliament against the enfranchisement of the Baron and his people; but we have not heard that they have refused the Baron's tax towards the maintenance of the Church. – *August, 1850.*

Samuel Roberts (1800-1885): Gweithiau Samuel Roberts, extracted
from The Chosen People: Wales and the Jews
edited by Grahame Davies
(Seren : 2002)

Rebellion at Llanidloes

Tuesday 30th. A lovely spring morning ushered in this eventful day, one ever to be remembered, by those who witnessed its proceedings, as perhaps the most momentous in the little town's history. At an early hour, information that a police force had arrived from London, leaked out through the domestics of the hotel, and it was also stated that they had come for the purpose of arresting the Chartist leaders. This intelligence spread rapidly through the town, and caused the greatest excitement among the members of the Political Union. After conferring together, the leaders determined to call a meeting of their supporters. A Chartist, armed with a long tin horn, was sent to parade the streets, and after each flourish of this musical instrument, he announced the fact that an assembly of the members of the Union would be held on the 'Long' Bridge. The tin horn, which is still preserved as a sacred relic in the family of the 'bugler', was styled by the Chartists the 'Horn of Liberty', while the soldiers who visited the town after the outbreak dubbed it the 'Chartists' Bugle'. In obedience to the summons numbers flocked to the bridge, where they were addressed from the parapet by one of the leaders, whose usual high-souled courage had deserted him upon the arrival of the London police, and had converted the confident leader into a timid suppliant for a mob's protection. While still appealing to the crowd around him in the most pathetic and touching manner, that they would not allow himself and his fellows to be given up to the minions of the law, messengers from different directions were seen approaching the spot. As soon as they came within hearing, they shouted out that three of their comrades had been arrested in front of the hotel by the London police. This startling intelligence threw the meeting into disorder, every one of its members seemed to think only of releasing their friends at once, and 'To the rescue!' pealed from lip to lip; and, as if galvanised, an instantaneous disorderly rush was made towards the Trewythen Arms to set their companions at liberty.

Strengthened by the arrival of the men sent by the Home Secretary, the magistrates assembled at the hotel, and decided upon arresting the individuals against whom the warrants were out; and, to be prepared for the worst, had sent the town crier to request the immediate presence at the Trewythen Arms of the special constables then in the town. Between forty and fifty obeyed the call, and, loitering before the inn, watching the proceedings, were the identical men whom the authorities were so anxious to apprehend: they were pointed out to the police, who at once took them into custody, and secured them inside the hotel. Upon this the tocsin of alarm was given, and the news of the arrest reached those assembled at the bridge in a very short time. This crowd, with their numbers swelled on the way, soon arrived in sight of the hotel, where they saw the police and special constables drawn up to receive them. The sight took them aback, but it was only the momentary impediment which dammed up the waters for a more impetuous rush. Without arms of some description, their great number was no match for the police and specials, armed with their staves of office. They accordingly withdrew for a few moments to procure whatever they could lay their hands on in the form of weapons – guns, staves, pikes, hay forks, sickles, and even spades were hastily seized by the excited and turbulent mob!

Some of the women who had joined the crowd kept instigating the men to attack the hotel – one old virago vowing that she would fight till she was knee-deep in blood, sooner than the Cockneys should take their prisoners out of the town. She, with others of her sex, gathered large heaps of stones, which they subsequently used in defacing and injuring the building which contained the prisoners. When the mob had thus armed themselves, the word 'Forward!' was given, and as soon as they were within hearing of the police, they imperatively demanded the release of their friends, which demand was of course refused. What took place during the next few minutes cannot be easily ascertained; both parties afterwards accused the other of commencing the fray. The special constables, many of whose acquaintances were among the crowd, were seen to give way on the approach of the Chartists, and to seek their safety either in the hotel, or by trusting to their legs. When their request was denied them, the mob set up a terrible shout, and pressed forward towards the door of the inn; the rioters asserting that the London police began the conflict by striking one of their number, which only exasperated them the more, and caused them to shout out for 'revenge!' as well as the release of the prisoners. They further state that the Ex-mayor, on finding that he was locked out, to ensure his own safety, suddenly appeared to sympathize with the mob, by crying out 'Chartists for ever,' and, with a stick which he had in his hand, broke the first pane of glass, thus initiating the mob in the work of destruction.

Edward Hamer: A Brief Account of the Chartist Outbreak
in Llanidloes in the year 1839 (1867)

Robert Owen

Robert Owen was born in 1771 and died in 1858, at the age of eighty-seven. He reached manhood at a time when the Industrial Revolution was just at the height of its first swift advance, and on the eve of the long war with France which vitally affected its course. As a man, he lived through the struggle with Jacobinism and with Napoleon, the economic crises and industrial disturbances which followed the Peace of 1815, the long national agitation for Parliamentary Reform, and the working-class movements, industrial and political, which followed the Reform Act of 1832. He outlived the Chartists, whose movement did not begin till he was an old man, and died in the very hey-day of mid-Victorian complacency and commercial expansion. And in most of the movements of his manhood's time he was a prominent and an influential actor.

Owen began life, as we shall see, with few advantages. He was born in a remote little town of central Wales, far from the bustle of the great commercial centres. His father was a tradesman in the town, and most of his relatives were farmers or tradesmen. He received only the ordinary education of the village school, from a master who could teach him little beyond the rudiments of reading and writing. At seven he became usher in his school; at nine he left school and went to work. But the spirit of adventure stirred in him. At ten he left Newtown, and came to London in search of fortune. From ten to eighteen he was shop-boy or assistant, first in Stamford, then in London, and last in Manchester. At eighteen, with a borrowed hundred pounds for his capital, he set up in business for himself as a manufacturer of the new textile machinery. Fortune and his personal qualities favoured him, and at twenty-nine he became the head of the great cotton mills at New Lanark, already among the biggest and best equipped in Great Britain.

G.D.H. Cole (1889-1959): Robert Owen

Character Forming

I was the youngest but one of a family of seven, – two of whom died young. The survivors, – Williams, Anne, and John, were older, and Richard was younger than myself. The principal adjacent estate was *Newtown Hall*, at the period of my birth and for a few years afterwards the property and residence of Sir John Powell Price, Bart.: – and my first recollection is of Sir John opening a glass door which divided my father's shop from the dwelling part of the house, and setting a bird flying towards us, saying there was something for the children's amusement, and they must take care of it.

This must have been shortly before he left his estate, I suppose from being in debt, for it soon passed into other hands. My next recollection is being in school in apartments in the mansion of this estate, and a Mr Thickness, or some such name, was the schoolmaster. I must have been sent young to school, – probably at between four and five years of age, – for I cannot remember first going there. But I recollect being very anxious to be first in school and first home, and the boys had always a race from the school to the town, and, being a fast runner, I was usually at home the first, and almost always the first at school in the morning. On one occasion my haste nearly cost me my life. I used to have for breakfast a basin of flummery, – a food prepared in Wales from flour, and eaten with milk, and which is usually given to children as the Scotch use oatmeal porridge. It is pleasant and nutritious, and is generally liked by young persons. I requested that this breakfast might be always ready when I returned from school, so that I might eat it speedily, in order to be the first back again to school. One morning, when about five years old, I ran home as usual from school, found my basin of flummery ready, and as I supposed sufficiently cooled for eating, for no heat appeared to arise from it. It had skinned over as when quite cold; but on my hastily taking a spoonful of it, I found it was quite scalding hot, the body of it retaining all its heat. The consequence was an instant fainting, from the stomach being scalded. In that state I remained so long, that my parents thought life was extinct. However, after a considerable period I revived; but from that day my stomach became incapable of digesting food, except the most simple and in small quantity at a time. This made me attend to the effects of different qualities of food on my changed constitution, and gave me the habit of close observation and of continual reflection; and I have always thought that this accident had a great influence in forming my character.

Robert Owen (1771-1857): The Life of Robert Owen

Davies the Ocean

At the outbreak of the Second World War, the Davies family at Llandinam and Gregynog was one of the richest in Wales, noted not only for its wealth but for its good works. Its philanthropy seemed limitless; it had funded an all-Wales campaign against the scourge of tuberculosis, established the world's first Chair of International Politics in Aberystwyth, bequeathed a priceless collection of French Impressionist paintings to the National Museum of Wales, provided the first pithead baths in Wales for miners, restored Owain Glyndŵr's Parliament House in Machynlleth, built garden villages and had poured money into a variety of religious and charitable causes. In the gathering gloom of the 1930s Lord Davies had campaigned vigorously, almost frenziedly, for a new international machinery which would make war obsolete, and had raised a Temple of Peace in Cardiff to give physical expression to his ideals. None of this would have been possible had not his grandsire been born with the strength of an ox and an indomitable will to succeed.

The founder of the dynasty was called Davies the Ocean after his Ocean group of collieries in the Rhondda and neighbouring valleys, and Davies Llandinam after the tiny Montgomeryshire village which he made a synonym for success. But he was also known by another name, Davies Top Sawyer, for at an early age his muscles were being hardened in the saw-pit on his father's hillside smallholding in Llandinam. When he died in 1890 his personal estate was valued at £404,424.10s.1d. He would have considered the penny important.

Herbert Williams: Davies the Ocean (1892)

A lasting memorial

'The home of Gwendoline and Margaret Davies is unique among country houses in Wales and I know of no parallel in England.'

Thomas Jones

These words, written in 1950 by my father, one of their closest advisers and friends, strike a note which still rings true, even though Gregynog itself has passed into the charge of the University of Wales and is now used by scores of people each year who never knew the two sisters who made it what it is. Gregynog, dedicated to the arts and to alleviating the social stresses of the time, was an emanation of these two women, a manifestation of their extraordinary qualities which even their intense personal shyness could not altogether mask.

So all who enjoy a brief sojourn under this roof may be glad to pause a moment to reflect on a remarkable story of an experiment in living, of how the two sisters dedicated themselves to spending their considerable inherited wealth for the benefit of mankind, but more particularly, for the benefit of their fellow countrymen in Wales. For comparison one might turn to Dartington Hall in Devon, under the munificent educational and artistic patronage of Leonard and Katherine Elmhirst. Yet the differences are profound, not least because the owners of Gregynog grew up under the influence of a strict Welsh Nonconformist tradition. In politics, the family was Liberal, another social characteristic which distanced them from what there was of county society in their day, while their great wealth made it difficult to sink inconspicuously into the rural middle class. Not fashionably intellectual and far from Bohemian, their education and wide travels made them nevertheless cultured, especially in music and painting, beyond most of their neighbours. It was their reaction to these and other more personal conditions which induced them to create Gregynog, which remains to this day part of their lasting memorial.

Eirene White: The Ladies of Gregynog (1985)

Without Fears or Tears

Though most of Llanbrynmair's inhabitants behaved throughout the War as if totally oblivious to the Nazi threat, we, as a family, were very conscious of the imminent danger, especially in the early years. I soon learnt to distinguish the sinister, undulating note of the German bombers returning over Mid-Wales after raids on Liverpool from the steady monotone of the Wellingtons and Halifaxes. Apart from one aircraft crashing in the hills above the river Cannon, a tributary of Nant yr Eira, a single-seater bursting into flames on the meadow below Ty-mawr farm in full view of us schoolchildren, and the convoys of jeeps, lorries and amphibious craft passing through just before the Normandy landings, the War could well have been fought on Mars. And apart from blackouts, ration-books, gas-masks, and the troop-trains to and from 55 Rgt R.A., Tonfannau, for most people in our self-centred and self-sufficient community, life continued virtually as it had always done, without many fears or tears.

Alun D.W. Owen: A Montgomeryshire Youth (2000)

Crash at Pennant Melangell, 1943

When they exhumed my airscrew
and stood it like a cross beside a wall
in photographed memorial –
then the valley recollected me.

Black and yellow,
droning back from clear French skies
my cameras were crammed with observations:
then mist slid shut
and trapped me in haphazard zig-zags
on the wrong side of a frosted pane.

As a schoolboy,
cribban banging at his back,
might panic-snivel near the end of day

I had no shame
at wishing anyone but me
to get last-minute tagged with this misfortune.

I eased down gently,
braced for the imagined shock
should fear collide with fact; yet praying for
the cloak to open
on a space to hide me from
the hunter without hunger hard behind.

The cloud's frayed edge gave way
and hillside colours stood up flat as paint –
my windscreen's bullet-proofing useless
with only false perspective's depth to catch me.

Michael Bartholomew-Biggs

Poet's note:

The legend of St Melangell tells how she defied a royal hunting party by sheltering a hare beneaeth her skirts while she prayed.

Cribban: a wooden token hung round the necks of schoolchildren in 19th century Wales, to mark them out for later punishment for speaking Welsh.

The Mowing Machine

The sound of the mowing machine is one of the most familiar sounds of the countryside in May and June. In the old days, hay-cutting was done with two-horse teams, a horse on either side of a central long shaft. As horses became tired, work with them at hay-cutting was done very early in the morning, before the heat of the day came. It was usual, here in Shropshire and the March country, for the mowing machines to be out in the meadows at four and four-thirty on a morning of early summer. Thus, most of the work was done by about eight o'clock; the wagoner and his team went away, leaving the field in those rectangles or squares of ever-decreasing size which gives a geometrical shape to the new-made swathes.

In these mechanical days, the mowing machines are pulled by tractors and can go on for as long as the poor human at the controls can carry on with the work. One-horse mowing machines are still used on the Welsh farms in the uplands, and often the farmer's wife is the worker of the mowing machine and the horse. She sits on the bouncing iron seat, with the long driving cords in her hand, while she takes the clattering machine over the steep-sided stone-walled fields. The children are, perhaps, in charge of some neighbour; the husband and the older boys are already at work raking into long mounds some other field which is a stage further on in the haymaking process. Large mounds of hay made on the field are a characteristic of the upland farms of Wales. These are often left for several weeks until carried into the loft or made into one great stack in a shaded corner of the field. Women of the Welsh farms have always been great workers.

Cledwyn Hughes (1920-1978): The House in the Cornfield

The Welshpool and Llanfair Railway

The slow and friendly, make-do-and-mend, wait-for-anyone Light Railway atmosphere was retained and embraced when revival came in recent years. However, new and novel features have emerged. When the hurried, unrelenting puffing up Dolarddyn bank is cut off, into grassy Castle station may coast a formidable continental o-8-oT, embellished with a plethora of outside fittings. Behind, rumbles a rake of match-board-sided end-balconied vintage Austrian coaches. A new generation crams the balconies; the basket-laden market-bound lilting Welsh wives have given way to camera-swinging, brochure-hugging, wide-eyed visitors with a variety of accents. Today, as the new W & L operates its rather remarkable service of busy trains in each summer season, one remembers that it is dependent on – and is a tribute to – the voluntary efforts of many well-wishers who have joined the preservation company, all drawn together in a pioneering spirit. Though there have been crises and disappointments and things have often seemed to be moving slowly, determination and perseverence have prevailed in the end. Throughout the railway's history this has been so . . .

Ralph Cartright and R.T. Russell: The Welshpool and Llanfair
Light Railway (1972)

With all my griefs in my arms

Above Montgomery, trudging the blade
of a gale blowing thunder from England,
our small family – a blond four-summers boy
whose whining hones my middle aged bad temper
to a saw; a baby daughter, one today,
who wont be carried but will not walk,
and 'Mum' whose love enfolds us all,
bending, laughing, cajoling joy
where we three'd settle for our selfish miseries.

It is a 'beauty spot', a tourists' plaque
describes the view for those whose eyes need names
and stories. From here you could see twelve counties,
all of Montgomery, most of Wales,
almost, it seems, to France. And up here
someone with a poet's heart sited
the county's cenotaph; a grey, unnatural
needles of stone piercing oblivion's eye.
Guiltily we sit on it, a shelter from the wind.

My son spills lemonade like a libation
while my daughter treads its boundaries in some
primal, gurgling rite. 'What's it for, Dad?
What's it do?' We mouth the usual platitudes
about the men who died, their bravery
our gratitude, the stupidity of war.
He's quickly bored and starts to fantasize
his own war games. Ptchoww! Kblamm!
He blasts the 'evil mutants' into smithereens . . .

Watching him my wife talks of conscription,
of mothers, lovers left at home,
and how we wouldn't let *him* go, we'd emigrate
or wound him in some way, bring on his asthma . . .
how anyway it wouldn't be like that again,
the mushroom cloud, the fire-next-time engulfing
everything, we'd all go up together, a family . . .
I look away, over England, down to the ford
where, since before the Romans came, young men

have fought to save their kin from strange invaders
with rough hands and tongues. I've boasted
that there's nothing I'd fight for, not flag,
religion or some abstract cause,
that choice a luxury my generation –
the first one for a thousand years
not swaddled with a bayonet – could afford.
But cradling my kids, here, on this stone,
I know that boast just empty words. I'd go,

like all the others did; not out of duty,
fear or pride, not for the bloodlust,
the excitement or the glory, not for
that fiction the movie-makers show,
but for love, that cruelest irony
the men who made this monument understood
and which, now, keeps it holy. Above
Montgomery, the wind streaming tears
down our faces, as we race the storm clouds

   booming in the east.

                                        Stewart Brown

Reflections

The parish of my childhood had more in common with the Middle
Ages than the mid-twentieth century, for it seemed almost
untouched by the great movements of modern British history.

142

Renaissance Man had clearly taken another route; Bell and Faraday might as well not have been born; and were it nor for the ubiquitous Raleigh Roadster and the single-track railway snaking along the valley bottom, the Industrial Revolution too was a century overdue. If Geoffrey Chaucer had lived in 1950s West Montgomeryshire instead of 1350s East London, he would have needed few amendments to his *Canterbury Tales*. This is why, no doubt, as a schoolboy learning about mediaeval life and literature. I felt a close affinity with the age and its characters. It required little imagination to conjure up the living conditions of those far-off pilgrims, because I experienced not dissimilar ones myself; no water mains; no sewerage system; no flush toilet; no bathroom; no kitchen; no gas; no electricity; no street lighting. And of course no television; no radio; and very limited access to 'civilisation', except by means of the occasional train from a station nearly two miles away along a twisting, country road. And yet ten miles away at Caersws two thousand years earlier, Roman legionaries had enjoyed luxuries that we could only dream about; central heating; hot baths; sophisticated sanitary arrangements; a clean water supply piped to the point of need and – straight roads!

Growing up in these primitive conditions left an indelible impression, for there is nothing romantic about the squalor of a rural slum. Those who drool over the bucolic charms of a 'country upbringing' cannot have experienced the remorseless buzz of summer insects nor the stench of faeces and urine, emptied weekly into the nearest stream or buried at the bottom of the garden. Those Roman soldiers would have been horrified at the disappearance of the amenities which they had taken for granted: it was as if some lost tribe in the fourth millennium had never experienced electricity, toilet soap or the telephone. And as a youngster I often reflected that those Romans would have been no less astonished at how slight an impact twenty centuries of civilisation had made on the native population. Indeed, to walk through the village square on a warm summer's Saturday evening after, say, a day at the seaside was not unlike making one's way through a fieldful of bullocks. Although one felt reasonably safe from physical assault, the collective dumb stare of a dozen yokels draped in various menacing postures on the Wynnstay bridge was an unnerving experience.

Alun. D.W. Owen: A Montgomeryshire Youth (2000)

Religion

Cloch Cennau/Cennau's Bell

Graham Hartill's poem is in three sequences and what follows is but the first of these.

The poem is concerned with a local saint, whose bell was excavated very close to the poet's former home at Llangenny and is preceeded by a passage from a guide to the church. A further passage from the guide follows the poem.

. . . directing her journey beyond the Severn and there meeting with certain woody places she made her request to the Prince of that country that she might be permitted to serve God in that solitude. His answer was that he was very willing to grant her request; but that the place did so swarm with serpents that neither men nor beasts could inhabit in it. Presently prostrating herself in fervent prayers to God, she obtained of him to change all the serpents and vipers there into stones. And to this day the stones in that Region do resemble the windings of Serpents through all the fields and villages . . .

Many years being spent by her in that solitary place, the holy Mayd returned to the seat of her nativity. Where, on the top of a hillock seated at the foot of a high mountain she made a little habitation for herself; and by her prayers obtained a spring there to flow out of the earth; which by the merits of the Holy Virgin afforded health to divers infirmities . . .

quoted in Notes on the Church and Parish of Llangenny,
Breconshire
by A. Raymond Hawkins

At Cennau's Well

What's my name?

Is it Cennau
    Keyne
        Keyne-wiri?

Whatever it was, I lost it across the estuary,
    I dropped it in that desart place the other side of the Severn,
        driving the serpents into the stones,
            deriving a kind of silent heaven

and now my name is just a place
    where jets and lorries clamber throughout my
        clouds, vibrate my bridges –

What's my name?
Is it Ceneu
    Keyna the Virgin
        Keyne?

and what's this place but a bigger body,
    a musculature of stones and beasts and jungled ridges?
        Whatever the name, I am now become this territory,
                        such as –

    foxhole,
        steppingstone,
            dyke,
                and ditch

I am become its bell, and my mouth will be buried,
    stuffed with leaf and twig, and rich with spider and
                       silver worm

my Father-God will always burn –

I am his bell and was rung before the mechanic, the
    metalled road, I sung when even the church
        was only a glade of stubble, a slab of stone with sockets
            for oil and water, a congregation of speechless rubble

I am a daughter of red-haired Brychan,
    daughter of burning –

        before the roadmap, almost before the furrow,
            I fixed this oratory (log for lintel, twisted branch for a
                                                roofridge –
            shoulder and backbone)

        the first smoke of the valley rose from my circle of stones

and now the fox winks at the window, an otter tumbles and churns
                                throughout my blood –

        I married this wood.

                        *   *   *

        I married this wood –

and beat my tongue in prayer like tempering bell-metal –
    slow-worm soul-work – beating a blade
        to hack a path
            through plagues of brambles,
        the body's jungles.

When I was south of the Severn, 'that desart place',
    I cured an epidemic, freezing the snakes into ammonites –
        but now I know that the codes of the corn and the river will twist
            and swell for ever, things will always fall in love
        with soil and water, crawl into bed with fire –

tonight, the lips of the fire and water whisper
    'Take and eat – this is my body'

but here there is no mirror
　　　　but rain-drenched rock, no love-lamp but the whinchat's
　　　　　　　　　　　　　　　　　breast –

I am Keyna the Virgin, and whisper my vespers to crowded sky
　　　　　　　　　　　　and wet black soil –

　　I am Cennau – a river in anger,
　　Keyne-wiri the buzzard,
　　　　　　　　　circling to rest.

　　　　　　　　*　　*　　*

The Lord does use me –

　I am his loophole
　　　foxhole
　　　　dyke
　　　　　and ditch

　　　　his pier
　　　　　steppingstone
　　　　　　ditch
　　　　　　　and shield

　　　　　his scrivener
　　　　　index
　　　　　　grapnel
　　　　　　　lifebuoy
　　　　　　　gin

So how can my service today be anything other than these –
　each letter a scribbled sun-stitch?

Slowly as serpents, the words uncurl,
　　the loin-pressure twists, unfurls
　　　and every phrase and cob in the drystone wall
　　　　that stammers across the pasture
　　knows that the code of the corn and the clouds, the law of
　　　　　　　　　　　genetic cities,

147

the clasp of the body's book,
will be broken,

the Word will awaken.

Graham Hartill

. . . But when the time of her consummation approached she saw in
a vision as it were, a fiery pillar, the base whereof was fixed on her
bed. Now her bed was the pavement strowed over with a few
branches of trees. And in this vision two Angels appeared to her,
one of which appeared to take off the sackcloth with which she
was covered and put on her a smock of fine linen, and over that a
tunick of purple, and last of all a mantell all woven with gold.

Therefore sending to her nephew Saint Cadocus, she said to
him 'This is the place above all others beloved by me; here my
memory shall be perpetuated. This place I will often visit in spirit
if it be permitted mee. And I am assured it shall be permitted mee
because our Lord has granted mee this place as a certain
inheritance.

My tomb shall lie a long time unknown . . .

from Cressy, quoted in 'Notes on the Church and Parish of
Llangenny, Breconshire', by A. Raymond Hawkins

The Patroness of Hares

From Llandderfel the old Sarn Helen, or Elen's Road, runs to
Llandrillo; and with a visit to this place may be combined one to
the Pennant of Melangell, who descended from this Elen and
her husband Maximus. Her mother was an Irish-woman.

The story goes that her father desired to marry her to a chief
under him, but either she disliked the man or the thought of
marriage, and determined to run away. Accordingly she found an
opportunity to escape, and secreted herself at Pennant, a lonely
and lovely spot at the head of the Tanat. Her story is represented
on the cornice of the carved oak screen of the church.

In this spot, sleeping on bare rock, she remained for fifteen
years. One day Brochwel, prince of Powys, was hunting and in

148

pursuit of a hare, when it escaped into a thicket and took refuge under the robe of a virgin of great beauty, whom the huntsman discovered. She faced and drove back the hounds. The huntsman then put his horn to his lips, and there it stuck as if glued. Upon this, up came the prince, and he at once granted a parcel of land to the saint, to serve as a sanctuary, and bade her found there a convent. This she did, and she lived in a cell, which still remains, though somewhat altered, at the east end of the church.

She was buried there, and fragments of her beautiful shrine, as it is believed, remain built into the walls, sufficient to allow of its reconstruction. The cell of S. Melangell is, as said, to the east of the church, and has no communication with it. It goes by the name of Cell-y-Bedd, or Cell of the Grave, and has a door and a window, and in this cell formerly stood her shrine.

Melangell is considered the patroness of hares, which are termed her lambs. Until the eighteenth century so strong was the superstition that no one in the parish would kill a hare, and even now, when a hare is pursued by hounds, boys will shout after it, 'God and Melangell be with thee!' and it is held that it will escape.

Sabine Baring-Gould (1834-1924): The Book of North Wales

Melangell

They call me saint.
They bless me and the hares they call my lambs,
here, in quietness of forest, fastness
of mountain wall.

Pennant is my place,
mellow paps the hills behind my home,
dappled cones sunlight plays upon,
with clouds dancing.

Fierce beasts were the waves
that tossed me, my landfall so
far west of here. Through winter's mire and frost
I struggled.

A carlin, hooped
in age gave me bowed wisdom, broth
in a dish of bone, simples and salves.
The body mends at last.

The spirit grows
to a glade's calm, chill of well water,
bannocks of coarse flour. I delve and hew,
Erin remembering:

Tanat rejoicing.
Then comes the summer of mallows and wild lupins
blue as streams on soft banks of seed,
the cry of the hunt,

the blare and wild
will of hounds, till through birches they come like a fire
running, a hare at my hem, a huntsman's horn singed
to his lips in a blister of sound.

They call it miracle,
and so it was, I, frozen in his prince's sight, never
having seen a man so like a god, a flame. His name is Brochwel
and I, a bride of Christ . . .

My hares, my lambs
are sweet velvet nutmegs. I have seen them dancing
in moonlight. At the *prie dieu* I leave posies
of white broom.

Maidens flock here,
craving this rule, this life I blend. As years
mount the arch of the sky, I kneel and whisper,
plaiting staunch cords of peace.

Glenda Beagan

Beuno

It seems clear that the royal family of Gwent issued from that of Powys, and this will explain the fact stated in the Life of Beuno that Bugi lived in Powysland by the Severn. His wife was named Beren, and she was the daughter of Llawdden. Their place of residence was Banhenig, near the river, the identity of which has not been fully established.

In their old age they had a son, whom they named Beuno, and sent him to Caerwent to be educated by Tangusius, who had probably succeeded Tathan as master of the college founded by Ynyr Gwent. Here he 'obtained a knowledge of all the Holy Scriptures; afterwards he learned the service of the Church and its rules, and took orders, and became a priest.'

Ynyr Gwent is represented as resigning his royal position and becoming, in his old age, a disciple of Beuno, to whom he granted lands in Ewyas. This is Llanfeuno, a chapelry now under Clodock, near Longtown.

Whilst here, Beuno heard that his father was ill, and committing the charge of his foundation in Ewyas to three of his disciples, he departed for Powys. 'And his father, after receiving the communion, making his confession, and rendering his end perfect, departed this life.'

Beuno now made a foundation in the township of his father, and set an acorn by the side of his grave, that grew in time to be a mighty oak, of which one branch curved down to the ground, and then rose again, 'and there was a part of this branch in the soil, as at present; and if an Englishman should pass between this branch and the trunk of the tree, he would immediately die; but should a Welshman go, he would in no way suffer.'

Thence Beuno went to visit Mawn, 'son of Brochwel' Ysgrythrog, king of Powys. The relationship is wrong. Mawn or Mawan was brother, and not son of Brochwel. Mawn granted him Aberrhiw, now Berriew, in Montgomeryshire, near Welshpool, where an upright stone remains, called Maen Beuno, marking the spot where Beuno is supposed to have preached to and instructed the people. It stands in the level land between the junction of the Luggy and the Severn, and the Rhiw and the same river, a little off the high road from Welshpool to Newtown.

One day, when Beuno was walking by the Severn, 'he heard a

voice on the other side of the river, inciting dogs to hunt a hare, and the voice was that of an Englishman, who shouted "Kergia! Kergia!" which in that language incited the hounds. And when Beuno heard the voice of the Englishman, he at once returned, and coming to his disciples, said to them, "My sons, put on your garments and your shoes, and let us leave this place, for the nation of the man with the strange language, whose cry I heard beyond the river urging on his hounds, will invade this place, and it will be theirs, and they will hold it as their possession".'

Then he commended his foundation at Berriew to a disciple named Rhithwlint, and departed to Meifod, where he remained with Tyssilio forty days and as many nights, and where he is said to have founded a church on land granted him by Cynan, son of Brochwel. However, he did not remain there. Two such shining lights as himself and Tyssilio could hardly abide together and Cynan gave him lands at Gwyddelwern, near Corwen, in Merionethshire.

S. Baring Gould and John Fisher: The Lives of the British Saints
(1907)

Long Mountain

A steep lane on Long Mountain
climbs beside Offa's earthwork,
twisted roots of an oak tree
leap like a boar from the ditch.
Pheasants in bronze finery
break cover, hint of an age
when borders had no meaning.

Beuno, with land at Berriew,
heard the shout of a huntsman
calling his dogs, – the strange tongue
of Mercian settlers. And there,
the shadow of a sentry
cursing the cold, dreaming of
honey cakes in *Valhalla*.

An arrow of geese returns
to Leighton's frozen marchland,
gods of the dyke hibernate
deep as coins under dark stones.
We are captured on camera,
three generations, our speech
sharpened on the wind's whetstone.

We rest at an iron gate,
behind us the western hills
stained with the sun's royal seal.
We migrate with ease across
borders, carry our culture
in a suitcase, fear pressing
like an ingrowing toenail.

Huw Jones

Eluned's Feast Day

In ancient times a man called Brychan was the nobly born and powerful ruler of this country of Brecknock. Indeed, it is from him that it is called Brycheiniog. The Welsh annals bear witness to the fact that he had twenty-four daughters. From their youth upwards they were all dedicated to the religious life, and they ended their days blissfully in this state of sanctity. There are still many churches in Wales which have the honour of being named after them. One is on the top of a hill in Brecknockshire, not far from the main castle of Brecon. It is called the church of Saint Eluned, after the name of the saintly virgin who on that spot refused the hand of an earthly ruler and married instead the King Eternal, thus triumphing in an ecstasy of self-denial.

Each year on the first day of August her feast-day is celebrated with great solemnity in this same place. On that day great crowds of ordinary folk assemble there from far and wide. Thanks to the merits of this blessed virgin, those who are suffering from maladies of any sort recover the health for which they pray. It seems to me that it is well worth my going into details of what happens almost every year at this feast of the virgin Eluned. You can see young men and maidens, some in the church itself, some in the churchyard and others in the dance which threads its way round the graves. They sing traditional songs, all of a sudden they collapse on the ground, and then those who, until now, have followed their leader peacefully as if in a trance, leap in the air as if seized by frenzy. In full view of the crowds they mime with their hands and feet whatever work they have done contrary to the commandment on sabbath days. You can see one man putting his hand to an [imaginary] plough, another goading on his oxen with a stick, and all as they go singing country airs, to lighten the tedium of their labour. This man is imitating a cobbler at his bench, that man over there is miming a tanner at his work. Here you see a girl pretending that she has a distaff in her hand, drawing out the thread with her hands, stretching it at arm's length, and then winding it back onto the spindle; another, as she trips along, fits the woof to the warp; a third tosses her shuttle, now this way, not that, from one hand to the other, and, with jerky gestures of her tiny tool, seems for all the world to be weaving cloth from the thread which she has prepared. When all is over, they enter the church. They are led up to the altar and there, as they make their oblation, you will be surprised to see them awaken from their trance and recover their normal composure. God in His mercy desireth not the death of a sinner, but rather that he may turn from his wickedness: and so, by taking part in these festivities, many men at once see and feel in their hearts the remission of their sins, and are absolved and pardoned.

Giraldus Cambrensis (1146-1223): The Journey Through Wales, translated by Lewis Thorpe

'The Silurian'

. . . many of the Metaphysical poets, who specialized in 'spiritual meanings within literal statements', were Welsh by origin, if not by residence – John Donne, the two Herberts, Thomas Traherne, Henry Vaughan – and though they generally wrote in English they expressed just the same luminous association of things seen and unseen. Among them the closest to his roots was Vaughan, 'The Silurian', whose whole life was spent in the ancient tribal territories of the Silures, along the lovely Usk in Powys. There he was born, there he ministered as a country doctor, and there he died, to be buried in the churchyard of Llansantffraid within sight of the river. The church was monstrously rebuilt by the Victorians, and a busy main road now separates it from the Usk, but still it is a magical sensation to stand there beside the Silurian's grave in the pale washed air of mid-Wales, looking across to the grand heights of Brycheiniog and remembering his poem about the afterworld:

They are all gone into the world of light!
And I alone sit ling'ring here;
Their very memory is fair and bright,
And my sad thoughts doth clear . . .

Jan Morris: Wales; Epic Views of a Small Country (1998)

The Retreate

Happy those early dayes! when I
Shin'd in my Angell-infancy.
Before I understood this place
Appointed for my second race,
Or taught my soul to fancy ought
But a white, Celestial thought,
When yet I had not walkt above
A mile, or two, from my first love,
And looking back (at that short space,)
Could see a glimpse of his bright-face;
When on some gilded Cloud, or flowre
My gazing soul would dwell an houre,
And in those waker glories spy
Some shadows of eternity;
Before I taught my tongue to wound
My Conscience with a sinfull sound,
Or had the black art to dispense
A sev'rall sinne to ev'ry sense,
But felt through all this fleshly dresse
Bright shootes of everlastingnesse.
    O how I long to travell back
And tread again that ancient track!
That I might once more reach that plaine,
Where first I left my glorious traine,
From whence th'Inglightned spirit sees
That shady City of Palme trees;
But (ah!) my soul with too much stay
Is drunk, and staggers in the way.
Some men a forward motion love,
But I by backward steps would move,
And when this dust falls to the urn
In that state I came return.

Henry Vaughan (1622-1295)

At the grave of Henry Vaughan

Above the voiceful windings of a river
An old green slab of simply graven stone
Shuns notice, overshadowed by a yew.
Here Vaughan lies dead, whose name flows on for ever.
Through pastures of the spirit washed with dew
And starlit with eternities unknown.
Here sleeps the Silurist; the loved physician;
The face that left no portraiture behind;
The skull that housed white angels and had vision
Of daybreak through the gateways of the mind.
 Here faith and mercy, wisdom and humility
 (Whose influence shall prevail for evermore)
 Shine. And this lowly grave tells Heaven's tranquillity
 And here stand I, a suppliant at the door.

Siegfried Sassoon (1886-1967)

At the grave of Henry Vaughan
The Commemoration Service at Llansantffraed-juxta-Usk

After the evensong,
And your hymn of a country far beyond the stars,
We gather in the churchyard by your grave
To pray for your eternal peace.
Even the Beacons look benign,
A figure of the everlasting arms,
In this hour before the necessary dark
That made your sparkling shine.

For you the world was veil
And sign, who read in waterfall and bird
A word that chided our blind busyness
And promised clarity and joy.
We use our subtler instruments
To deconstruct its text to emptiness,
Caught between fear of chaos and the terror
Of insignificant order.

We find ourselves the author,
Whichever Book we open. We contrive
To keep the faith we share with you alive
By love of an unproven ghost
Who casts the shadows of our fiction.
We spell for you our twilight praise and prayer
Whose flint was struck for our illumination
And glimpse His signature.

Joseph P. Clancy

Love

George Herbert is thought to have been born in Montgomery Castle in April 1593, the fifth son of Sir Richard Herbert and Lady Magdalen Herbert.

Love bade me welcome; yet my soul drew back,
    Guilty of dust and sin.
But quick-eyed Love, observing me grow slack
    From my first entrance in,
Drew nearer to me, sweetly questioning
    If I lacked anything.

'A guest,' I answered, 'worthy to be here.'
    Love said, 'You shall be he.'
'I, the unkind, the ungrateful? Ah, my dear,
    I cannot look on Thee.'
Love took my hand, and smiling, did reply,
    'Who made the eyes but I?'

'Truth, Lord, but I have marred them: let my shame
    Go where it doth deserve.'
'And know you not,' says Love, 'who bore the blame?'
    'My dear, then I will serve.'
'You must sit down,' says Love, 'and taste my meat.'
    So I did sit and eat.

George Herbert (1593-1633)

William Morgan

A Welshman was working in the solitude of Llanrhaeadr, a secluded village nestling in one of the romantic ravines which skirt the eastern slopes of the Berwyn. William Morgan was engaged in translating the Bible into Welsh. Versions of parts of it had already been published, but the Welsh was so uncouth that they could never have become popular. Morgan represents, at its best, the prose which always comes at the end of a golden period of poetry. His style is natural and clear, and contains an echo of the departing music of the dying literature of the previous century. The new Bible was, in parts, a re-construction of the earlier versions of William Salesbury; and Thomas Huet, and Bishop Richard Davies, and it was revised by Bishop Parry, when the new edition, still the authorised edition, was published in 1620. But it is substantially William Morgan's work; and since its publication in 1588, its influence over the life and thought of every successive generation has increased until this day.

William Morgan was the son of a tenant who lived in one of the glens of the Conwy, on the estate of Sir John Wynn of Gwydir. His devotion to his great task of translating the Bible at Llanrhaeadr, and his fearless championship of the Church against its spoilers as bishop of St Asaph, contrasts forcibly with the apathy of the mass of the clergy and with the selfishness of many of the bishops of his day.

O.M. Edwards (1858-1920): Wales

Llanrhaeadr-ym-Mochnant

This is where he sought God,
And found him? The centuries
Have been content to follow
Down passages of serene prose.

There is no portrait of him
But in the gallery of
The imagination: a brow
With the hair's feathers

159

Spilled on it? A cheek
Too hollow? Rows of teeth
Broken on the unmanageable bone

Of language? In this small room
By the river expiating the sin
Of his namesake?
                    The smooth words
Over which his mind flowed
Have become an heirloom. Beauty
Is how you say it, and the truth
Like this mountain-born torrent,
Is content to hurry
Not too furiously by.

                                            R.S. Thomas (1913-2000)

The Power of the Cock

Upon *Christmas* day, about three o'clock in the morning, most of
the parishioners assembled in church, and after prayers and a
sermon, continued there singing psalms and hymns with great
devotion till broad day; and if, through age or infirmity, any were
disabled from attending, they never failed having prayers at home,
and carols on our SAVIOUR'S nativity. The former part of the
custom is still preserved; but too often perverted into
intemperance. This act of devotion is called *Plygan*, or the *Crowing
of the Cock*. It has been a general belief among the superstitious,
that instantly,

                    at his warning,
    Whether in sea or fire, in earth or air,
    Th'extravagant and erring spirit hies
    To his confine.

But during the holy season, the Cock was supposed to exert his
power throughout the night; from which, undoubtedly, originated
the *Welsh* word *Plygan*, as applied to this custom. Accordingly,
Shakespeare finely described this old opinion:

Some say, that ever 'gainst that season comes
Wherein our SAVIOUR'S birth is celebrated,
The bird of dawning singeth all night long:
And then, they say, no spirit walks abroad:
The nights are wholesome: then no planets strike:
No fairy takes: no witch hath power to charm,
So hallowed and so gracious is the time.

Thomas Pennant (1726-1798): Tours in Wales

The Plygain

I heard the Reverend Geraint Vaughan-Jones, vicar of Mallwyd, near Machynlleth, talking about the *Plygain* on a radio programme, so I rang him up. He explained that the *Plygain* was held during the special evening service, usually in the first couple of weeks in January, and was very well attended. 'After the third collect I call *Plygain* and people come forward to sing – in Welsh, of course. The whole thing is impromptu. They sing in small groups, mostly trios and quartets, usually families, who tend to 'own' carols and woe betide anyone else who tries to sing them. They always sing unaccompanied. Sometimes they're a bit bashful and there's a lull so I call for a regular hymn while they sort themselves out. On a really good night there can be up to thirty-five or forty carols. It can go on for a couple of hours.'

Originally this service was held long before dawn on Christmas Day; the word *plygain* is Welsh for 'cock crow'. People would walk through the night to be at church by the appointed time, perhaps 4 or 5 o'clock, to sing their carols by candlelight. Until the turn of the century the custom was observed all over Wales, in many places preceded by torchlight processions and lively Christmas Eve parties. Today it survives in a small area of Mid Wales , and at a less demanding time of day.

Brian Shuel: Guide to Traditional Customs of Britain (1985)

For the Quakers of Montgomeryshire

I

We are a people
cold with creeds,
harried prey
of hireling priests.

In a broad white hat
and leather breeches
a preacher rides
from crowded fells,
his followers, like ferns,
shaking in the wind.

II Meifod

Brethren,
a Fox in sheep's clothing
leads our flock astray.

Trust not those
who go naked for a sign,
set sacrament aside
and boast of inward light.

At Coed Cowryd,
cobblers, blacksmiths
and even women preach.
Pray for their salvation.

III Welshpool

Snow on the mountain
sills barred with ice.

We sleep in straw
and dirt, snared
for refusing the Oath,

dragged from our beds
to lie with robbers,
walked in chains
to Quarter Sessions.

Our allegiance is to one
who has no need of oath
nor tithe, nor sermons blabbed
like ballads at a fair.

Now we, like Paul, must wait.
The day is coming
when the faithful will be
as snow on the mountain.

IV Dolobran Hall

Spiders case
this secret kingdom,
moonlight flirts
with boarded windows.

Breathless now
the Foundry bellows,
slack and mute
the heavy chains.

Empty paths that led
to grace, man's estate
lost in grass.

V Esgairgoch

They came to claim
the common land,
left open gates
paths cut back.

In a steep half-acre
pitted by cattle,
their bones were planted
under clouds of hawthorn.

A small field, lost
among the nine and ninety.

Huw Jones

Persecution

. . . though Richard Davies escaped much of the bitterness of suffering, in many parts of Wales Friends suffered many imprisonments, the breaking up of their meetings, and the spoiling of their goods.

At one place a meeting was broken up by people who came out of the church, but the constable took the preacher away to the town, and here the preacher continued his discourse and was attentively listened to. After his sermon the man reverently knelt down to pray, but just then the servants of the parish priest came up, making a great noise with rattles, a candlestick, and a frying-pan. They sought to drown the voice of the man at prayer, in which they easily succeeded. The party admitted that they had been 'set on' to do this, and even the priest's maid threw water in the faces of the Friends. The priest eventually secured the arrest of seven of the Friends, and though several of the priest's hearers attested that they saw nothing done by the Quakers but what was peaceable and orderly, the justices committed the whole seven to the common gaol till the next assizes, which were not due for another five months. No breach of the law could be proved against the men at the assizes, but because they came before the judge with their hats on they were each sentenced to three months imprisonment for contempt of court.

H.D. Phillips: The Early Quakers in Wales (1912)

Falsehoods

Vavasor Powell, an eminent Nonconformist preacher of the seventeenth century, although born out of Montgomeryshire, was closely connected with the county by descent and marriage, as well as residence within it for some years, and is intimately associated with the early history of its Nonconformity. He was born at Knucklas, Radnorshire, in the year 1617. His father, Richard Powell, belonged to an ancient Welsh family who had lived in that neighbourhood a hundred years before him. His mother was of the Vavasors, a family of great antiquity that came from Yorkshire into Wales. His bitter enemies (of whom his sturdy and energetic Nonconformity produced many) have endeavoured to throw discredit upon his origin, as well as upon every action of his life. Thus Anthony Wood, in his *Athenæ Oxonienses*, with ill-concealed spite, says: –

> Vavasor Powell having often told his friends and the brethren, not without boasting, that he was once a member of Jesus College in Oxon, I shall therefore upon his word number him among these writers. Be it known, therefore, that this person, who was famous in his generation for his ill name among those that were not of his opinion, was born in the Borough of Knucklas, in Radnorshre, son of Richard Howell, an Ale-keeper there, by Penelope, his wife, daughter of William Vavasor, of Newtown, in Montgromeryshire. He was brought up a scholar, saith the publisher of his Life, but the writer of *Strena Vavasoriensis* tells us that his employment was to walk guest's horses, by which finding no great gain at such a petty Ale-house, he was elevated in his thoughts for highter preferment, and so became a Hostler (I would say Groom) to Mr Isaac Thomas, an Innkeeper and Mercer in Bishop's Castle in Shropshire.

The above statement as to the occupation of Powell's father, and the other depreciating remarks which follow, are copied from *Strena Vavasoriensis*, or *Hue and Cry*, &c., a scurrilous book written by one Alexander Griffiths, and published about 1652 while Powell was in prison. It is almost entirely a tissue of calumnious falsehoods, to refute which Charles Lloyd of Dolobran, the Rev.

James Quarrell, and others, in 1653, published *Examen et Purgamen Vavasoris*. The author of the *Strena* describes Powell's father as 'a poor Ale-man and Badger of Oatmeal'. His grandfather, William Vavasor, was the son of Andrew Vavasor, sheriff of Montgomeryshire in 1563, and was himself High Constable of the Hundred of Newtown, 39 Eliz. (1596). Walker *(Sufferings of the Clergy)* says that Powell became 'a Schoolmaster, and at length a preacher at Clun,' and charges him with having entered the church by means of forged orders, – a charge for which there seems not to have been a particle of foundation.

Richard Williams: Montgomeryshire Worthies (1894)

Anne Griffiths

It was on the farm called Dolwar Fach, near Llanfyllin in Powys, that this unlikely genius was called to her fulfilment. The property remains much as it was then, an isolated but comfortable smallholding of the lowlands, very simple still, with pigs and geese and innumerable dogs, and a few relics of the hymn-writer still in the front parlour, where pilgrims come from all over the world to sign their names reverently in the visitors' book. Until her marriage to a neighbouring farmer Anne Griffiths ran this place herself, helped only by an illiterate companion, Ruth Evans, and her poems came to her as she worked in the fields – when the inspiration came she would throw herself to the ground with cries of wonder. She never committed the words to paper, and they were preserved, we are assured, only by the memory of Ruth Evans, who dictated them after the poet's death (in childbirth, aged 29, in 1805). They are hymns of an almost erotic abandonment, in which all Anne Griffiths's emotions are sublimated in her passionate yearning for Christ, and she welcomes the Godhead, like poor Mari Evan the prophetess of Ardudwy, all but physically as her lover – *Oh! to linger all my life-time in his love!*

Jan Morris: Wales: Epic Views of a Small Country (1998)

Lo, Between the Myrtles

Lo, between the myrtles standing,
One who merits well my love,
Though His worth I guess but dimly,
High all earthly things above;
    Happy morning
When at last I see him clear!

Rose of Sharon, so men name Him;
White and red His cheeks adorn;
Store untold of earthly treasure
Will His merit put to scorn;
    Friends of sinners,
He their pilot o'er the deep.

What can weigh with me henceforward
All the idols of the earth?
One and all I here proclaim them,
Matched with Jesus, nothing worth;
    O to rest me
All my lifetime in His love!

Ann Griffiths (1776-1805),
translated from the Welsh by Sir H. Idris Bell

The Monastery

The monastery at Capel-y-ffin, four miles north-west of Llanthony in the valley of Ewyas, was built in the 1860's by the famous Anglican preacher known as Father Ignatius. His idea was to revive the Benedictine monastic life in the Church of England, but owing to a variety of causes, important among which were his frequently prolonged absences on preaching tours to collect money and the eccentric and fantastic version of the Benedictine Rule which he concocted, the project had been a failure, so that when he died in 1908 there were only three of his monks left and they without money or the approval of their Anglican superiors. These three joined the more recently founded and more successful Anglican Benedictine Abbey on Caldy Island, near Tenby, and so the buildings at Capel became part of the property of that community. The Benedictines of Caldy joined the Roman Church in a body in 1913 and that was how we came to know them. When therefore early in 1924 we heard that they had a disused monastery in the Black Mountains and were willing to consider letting us (i.e. the Ditchling Guild) have the place as their tenants, I and another brother went to inspect and report. It was a weirdly exciting business. We arrived about midnight in deep snow having with great difficulty hired a motor car at Abergavenny fifteen miles away. It seemed as though God alone could know where we had got to, if anywhere. For miles and miles we had been driving slowly and dangerously up a narrow and very rough mountain lane and then we arrived at that dark and almost uninhabited and uninhabitable place.

Eric Gill (1882-1940): Autobiography

Old Tynoro

Harri wasn't paying much attention to the sermon. The wavering voice flowed through his head, and the meaningless words rattled like marbles against the closed doors of his mind. The fault was not the preacher's. Harri was here in the family pew at Bethel on a Sunday morning not because Tynoro Thomas was a good preacher but because he was a man.

Harri wasn't a keen chapel-goer, despite the frequent blandishments of his father. But the Reverend Tynoro Thomas's regular visits to Lleifior during his mother's illness had pricked his conscience. Of course, some of Bethel's members, those who could never be silenced, said that old Tynoro visited Lleifior more often than any other home because the Lleifior family were 'important people'. If that were true, Harri disapproved.

But after all, who had the right to find fault with the old boy? He relied in his preaching on platitudes, went about his pastoral duties less frequently, and had no way with the young people . . . Heck, they had a cheek to pick holes in him. He was getting old, he was tired, he was, naturally, in the things of the mind, behind the times. But after all, he'd given of his best. He'd devoted his life to his religion, and unsparingly, and still did so in his own old-fashioned way. Old Tynoro didn't work union hours, but according to the dictates of conscience, and for lower wages than Wil James got. For a moment, the injustice of it seared Harry's conscience. Then he took his conscience off elsewhere.

What would old Tynoro say, he wondered, if he knew that he was becoming a bit of a Communist? Seldom, did the old boy venture into politics from the pulpit, but when he did, it was Godless Communism that came in for it every time. Hitler had been the target for a while during the war, but these days it was Stalin and his cronies who came under the lash. What would he say, Harri wondered, if he knew at this moment that the son of his wealthy senior deacon and the scion of Lleifior was mixing with one of Stalin's wenches?

Islwyn Ffowc Elis: Cysgod y Cryman (Shadow of the Sickle), translated by Meic Stephens